THE
PRECARIOUS
WALK

THE PRECARIOUS WALK

Essays from Sand & Sky

Phyllis Barber

TORREY HOUSE PRESS

Salt Lake City • Torrey

First Torrey House Press Edition, May 2022
Copyright © 2022 by Phyllis Barber

Published by Torrey House Press
Salt Lake City, Utah
www.torreyhouse.org

International Standard Book Number: 978-1-948814-59-1
E-book ISBN: 978-1-948814-60-7
Library of Congress Control Number: 201941552

Cover art by Hallie Rose Taylor
Cover design by Kathleen Metcalf
Interior design by Rachel Buck-Cockayne
Distributed to the trade by Consortium Book Sales and Distribution

Torrey House Press offices in Salt Lake City sit on the homelands of Ute, Goshute, Shoshone, and Paiute nations. Offices in Torrey are on the homelands of Southern Paiute, Ute, and Navajo nations.

To Those Who Wish to Be Read

Contents

Part One ○ In the Desert

Part Two ○ Beyond the Desert

Part One

IN THE DESERT

OH, SAY CAN YOU SEE?

O

Over the radio microphone, into the nation's and FDR's ears, my grandma sang "The Star-Spangled Banner." "Oh, say can you see," she sang, the woman who ironed for nickels and dimes. Everybody in Boulder City, Nevada, recommended her for the dam's dedication program. They'd heard her sing at funerals, beautifully enough to make them cry even more than they might have. "What so proudly we hail."

A big black open car full of VIPs delivered her home from the ceremony. She probably waved goodbye longer than those men expected, as if it were the last time she'd be waving goodbye—her hand pausing in the air, both wanting to push the car along and wanting to keep it close to her.

I can see her there, maybe because I somehow feel connected to that woman and her difficult life, dressed in her Sunday dress, most likely black cotton, with low, broad-heeled shoes. She must have sung by the memorial, in between those stylized statues—massively chested men wearing tall stiff wings pointing skyward. Her notes must have hovered high above the Colorado from where she stood on top of Hoover Dam, now diverting water to be used for the benefit of humankind. (I hope those ninety-six men who died building the dam were given fluffier wings by the purveyor of angel equipment. Those bronze wings wouldn't lift anybody anywhere.)

I remember that dam and the stories about Grandma. But there was something else about growing up in the Mojave Desert that will never leave my mind—a rip in the sky, a test, a gash that showed the sky's insides for a minute. I thought about my Band-Aid box when I saw it—a funny thing to think about then, but I did. I could never have unwrapped enough Band-Aids to patch the desert even if I had pulled the red string exactly down the side crease without tearing into the flat side of the paper where the red letters are printed. After that first fire-in-the-blank-sky passed, the heaven's blood and the earth's dust made a big cloud, a busy one that drifts over my mind more often than I'd like.

But back to the dam. I got my first chance at swearing because of Hoover Dam—I went to the dam to get some dam water. I asked the dam man for some of his dam water and the dam man said no. Damns were frowned on at home, so I chanted the forbidden whenever I could, with a flourish, making sure Mama and Daddy heard.

Actually, everybody called it Boulder Dam until Congress restored the name Hoover in 1947, this in memory of Herbert Hoover, the Great Engineer. He got the whole thing started when he was secretary of commerce in 1921, way before the Depression and the WPA ever happened. He was head of the Colorado River Commission that signed a compact between the upper and lower basins of the affected states and chaired talks about what needed to be done with that unruly river. Hoover Dam. That was the answer.

At one time or another, people our family knew—the boasters, we called them—talked about jumping off or sliding down the curving concrete, but nobody did it except one time a man from New York did. His note said he lost his money gambling in Las Vegas and that nothing mattered anyway.

"He looked like a mass of jelly," Uncle Tommy, who was an electrician on the dam, said.

"Could you see his face at all?" I asked.

"It was like a leaky puzzle, liquid in the cracks."

I wanted to ask more but Aunt Grace changed the subject.

Whenever anybody came to visit we always took them to see the dam. Down to Black Canyon, down to 120 degrees in the shade where heat ricocheted off sizzling boulders. You could even see the level of heat.

Every time, we stopped at the memorial on the Nevada side. The two bronzed angels stood guard over a message: "It is fitting that the flag of our country should fly in honor of those men . . . inspired by a vision of lonely lands made fruitful." My sister Elaine said that some of them fell off scaffolds into wet, pouring cement. Concrete soup. I always looked to see if a hand or a foot stuck out anywhere in the dam and checked for lumps on the smooth surface, though I've since heard that the dam was built in a series of forms—building blocks—that were only three feet deep. If somebody fell into three feet of most anything, they could be found, I think, though it's more interesting to look for lumps.

The cloud, I remember, was lumpy itself: swollen and bulging. I've seen many gatherings of clouds in my life—lambs, potatoes, even alligators—but I saw only one like that bulging mushroom. Its cap reminded me of the North Wind, the puffy-cheeked one who bets with the Sun and blows fiercely to get coats off people's backs. Instead of sky and trees, it blew into the earth and got everything back in its face—sand, splintered tumbleweeds, thousands of years of rocks battering their own kind, crashing, colliding against each other, the dry desert silt, jaggedly rising from the ribboned gullies and rain patterns in the sand, rising into a cloud that looked like a mushroom or the North Wind puffing for all of its worth.

○

My father was proud of Hoover Dam. He helped build it, driving trucks, hauling fill. He also loved the desert. Mama never thought much of it, not much at all.

"Herman, it's so hot here, so dusty. No creeks, no greenery. It's not human to live here." My daddy always smiled when she started in. I liked his smile when she seemed unhappy, not sure what it meant, but somehow it was reassuring.

"Herman, can't we move before it's too late?"

Daddy never argued this subject. He just reminded Mama of his mother, the grandma who sang, and how she saved her family with a letter to her shirttail relative: "Can't find work. We've tried everything in the Great Basin—farming in Idaho, mining in Nevada, selling shoes in Utah. Thought you might have a place for my husband and sons helping on that big new dam."

"It seemed like we were heading for Mecca, it did," he used to say. "All those mirages on the highway and our tires never getting wet. Sunshine, open-armed skies, and promises."

"Promises? Of what?" Mama would ask. "How can you cultivate rocks in Black Canyon, Hoover Dam cement, the sage, the yucca?"

"I have a job, a wife, three children, and an address," he said. "God bless the government."

Once Mama left the desert and the dam, the time when my father put on his navy uniform with the brass buttons to go sailing in the Pacific during World War II, but she wasn't treated as she should have been. Daddy always reminded her of that fact. Mother thought her relatives would help out with me and Elaine when she moved to Idaho Falls, Idaho, but all extra hands were needed for milking, haying, harvesting potatoes.

"I'm sorry, but—" they all said.

Mama taught school—six grades in one room. She was tired at night when she picked me up from the scratch-and-bite nursery school for war orphans. She didn't talk much then, so I looked for Daddy under the covers, under the bed, and in the bathtub.

"Why did Daddy go away? Is he coming back?"

Mama read letters to us, words like China, Okinawa, kamikaze, Battleship *Missouri*, destroyers, phrases like "I miss you," "When the war is over," and "When we get back home to Boulder City, I'll roll down Administration Hill with my girls."

Rolling. Me rolling, repeating my face to the green grass. Laughing. Turning. All the way to the bottom. The cloud rolled, too, repeating itself to the open sky. And deep inside the busy cloud, a fire burned. Not a bonfire, but a tall fire hedged by a column of jumbled whites, browns, and grays. A thick fire mostly hidden but not quite. Black smoke twisted away from the fire, sometimes losing itself in the confusion, sometimes slithering out into the blue. The cloud burned, scarring its belly, melting its insides with red and yellow while it rolled over and over in the same place.

We pass Administration Hill every time we drive to the dam to go on what seemed like the world's longest elevator ride, dropping down deep into the stomach, the belly of Hoover, to the hum of big red generators with white round lights on top.

The guide always talked about kilowatts, power to southern California, and spillover precautions. I watched the ant tractors and drivers circling the generators stories below while he explained.

"Now, if you'll follow me, we'll go directly into the Nevada diversion tunnel," a voice from a bullhorn said. Our feet echoed through a dripping cave. "Man-blasted," the voice said.

Water roared through a giant gray penstock (the guide called it) under the square observation room. I barely heard his speech there was so much noise from the water traveling through the pipe on which the room sat, the pipe much bigger than the little room where we stood and listened, arms folded, slightly nervous. He pointed to yellow, red, blue, and green lines on a painted chart under a green metal lampshade. Outside the glass, chicken-wired window, a man balanced on a catwalk to check bolts twice his size. The room trembled. The water rushed. I was glad I didn't have to tightrope catwalks and check pipes as big as the world.

"If you'll step this way, I'll lead you now to the base of the dam. Watch your step, ladies and gentlemen."

Outside, we looked up, up, everywhere up. Big cables stretched across, miles overhead—cables that lowered tons of railroad cars onto the tracks where we stood. I moved my toe quickly at the thought. Over the edge of the wall, the Colorado whirled green pools into white foam.

One time I told my mother the river must be mad.

"Rivers don't get angry," she said.

"This one does. It doesn't like going through all those tunnels and generators. It would suck me down forever if I fell in."

"You won't fall in. Mother's here to protect you."

Reassured, I ran from the wall to the center point where I could spread-eagle across two states.

"Ma'am," blared the bullhorn, "will you kindly keep your child with the tour group?"

My mother jerked me back into Arizona and told me to stop wandering off.

After the tour, back at the top of the dam, Uncle Tommy scooped six-year-old me into his arms. The temperature must have been 128 degrees that day.

"See, honey. See the steepest, longest slide on earth." He not only held me up but leaned me over the edge to see better.

"Uncle Tommy. Put me down." I kicked and squirmed.

"Not yet, honey. Look at the big river down there. We stopped that river. We did it. Look. We harnessed it. That's where you were a few minutes ago. See the railroad tracks?" He held me with only one arm as he pointed.

"Uncle Tommy. Put me down. Please. I don't like to look

there." My head buried into his gray uniform but got stopped at the metal numbers on his badge.

"Ah, come on honey. Uncle Tommy wouldn't let anything happen to you." He still held me so I could see over the edge.

"Let me down. Let me down."

"Gee. Why are you so upset? I wouldn't—"

I ran away from his words, away to the car that boiled the closest two feet of air around its metal surface. The door handle was untouchable, unopenable. I couldn't hide away to cry. I had to do it in the air, on top of that dam, in front of people from Manila, Cheyenne, and Pittsburgh.

○

I used to wonder if there had been devils in that redfire cloud. My mother sometimes talked about how devils like fire and red and gambling, even how the world will end by fire because of them. I imagined horns balancing on top of their red caps that buttoned tight, holding all that cunning close between their ears while they rolled and tumbled in the churning clouds, while the fire burned yellow and red at the center and in my eyes.

One night, I dreamed that Uncle Tommy and my mother balanced a bed on the overhead cables, thousands of feet above concrete and water.

"You have disobeyed again," Mama said. "Always running off."

"I'm sorry."

"You'll have to sleep out there tonight, girl. Maybe you'll learn to listen."

"Please, Mother. Not at the dam. I'll be good. I'll listen. I won't go away without telling you ever again."

"Just climb up the ladder, honey," said Uncle Tommy. "Nothing to worry about."

"Please, no," I said as I climbed the ladder up, up, high above the scenic viewpoint where tourists said "ooh" and "ahhh." The wind blew, the cables rose and fell and twirled jump rope. I wore my blue furry Donald Duck slippers and my rosy chenille bath-robe, and I put one foot and then another foot ahead. For a min-ute I walked on the wind and wasn't afraid. Then I got to the creaking bed that tilted with every shift in weight.

"Rock-a-bye baby," Mama sang from the cliff's edge. "Hush-a-bye." Uncle Tommy accompanied her on his trumpet.

The bed slipped. The bedsprings scraped over the cables, fingernails on a blackboard, slipping one by one.

"Mama," I screamed.

Mama leaned as far out over the edge as she could while Uncle Tommy held her knees. We stretched for each other. Like long, rubbery, airless balloons we stretched and stretched, arch-ing, reaching, trying to connect.

"Hold me, Mama."

Our fingertips only pointed at each other as I passed.

I tried to make a sail out of the quilt. I stood up to catch the wind but couldn't keep my balance. One Donald Duck slip-per, followed by the other, followed by me in rose chenille, sailed through the night toward the dam to get some dam water from the dam man.

○

After it mushroomed, the cloud broke apart and dotted the sky, and I thought of the time I climbed a leafless tree. Instead of watching where I was going, I talked to Rocky, my dog, who jumped and yelped at the bottom. Someone else had broken the twig that raked my cheek, that beaded the slash with red. A necklace of red pearls. Dot dash dot. A design that stared at me in the mirror until it got better and faded away just like the cloud did. Where does something go when it's finished doing what it's supposed to do? I wonder, I do, but I have no answer to that question. For now, I'll just be glad that everybody wants to see the dam. It's famous. Our town was built to build the dam. People from all over the world come to see it.

One day when I was about ten, another big black car, open and full of important men, drove through Boulder City. Flags stuck out on both sides of the windshield, rippling. I tried every possible angle to see Ike, running around legs, pushing through to openings but finding none. I was missing everything. Everybody who had closed shop and home for the afternoon was crowding to see Ike, too.

"Daddy, hold me up so I can see."

His dark blue uniformed arms full of baby brother, he pointed to the sill of Central Market's picture window. Stacks of returnable glass bottles towered behind the pane and wiggled every time a reflected parade watcher moved. I climbed to the ledge as the fire engine and two police cars sirened past. Even standing there, I could see only flashing red lights, the backs of heads, and an occasional helium balloon drifting, ownerless.

"Daddy. I can't see."

Somehow, he managed to pick me up in time. Ike, his uniform dotted with brass and ribbons, looked just like the newsreel pictures at the Boulder Theater. He smiled and waved just like on the newsreel, too. I didn't need to see him after all. I already knew.

I liked the high school band best. The flags and the band.

"Children," my daddy said at the dinner table that night. "You are lucky to live in America." His blue eyes moistened as they always did when he talked about God and country. We all knelt by our chairs, and Daddy said, "We thank thee for such men as General Eisenhower to lead our great country. Bless our friends and relatives. Help us to live in peace. In the name of Jesus Christ, amen."

I saw Ike again on the newsreel several weeks later. He was still waving and smiling, framed by the granite-like building blocks of the dam. He didn't look too big next to the dam. Neither did his friends.

o

One morning, about five o'clock, our gray Plymouth drove in the opposite direction from the dam toward Las Vegas to a dirt road just before Railroad Pass where Uncle Tommy played trumpet on Saturday night. Elaine and I kept warm under a friendship quilt and read the embroidered names of Mama's old friends, waiting.

"It's time," Daddy said. "Watch. Don't miss this. We should be able to see everything, even if it is seventy-five miles away."

We waited some more, eating apples and crackers.

"It's got to be time," he said.

My neck cramped. I looked at the sunrise.

"There it is, there it is," he yelled.

I saw the flash, but mostly my father's face and his brass buttons that seemed to glow red for one instant.

"That's how I came home to you, everybody. Just look at that power."

The cloud flowered, mushroomed, turned itself inside out, and poured into the sky. Red fire burned in the middle of browns and grays, colors that hid the red almost. But it was there—the fire burning at the center, the fire that charred the North Wind's puffed cheeks and squeezed eyes until it blew itself away, trailing black smoke and its pride. It was there in the middle of the rising columns of earth and clouds boiling over, clouds bursting into clouds, whipping themselves inside out, changing colors over and over. Red, yellow, and black, colors from the fire. Gray, brown, and beige—sand from the desert floor, Daddy said.

And then the picture blurred at its edges, unfocused itself into other shapes—smoky arches, long floating strings. In no time at all, everything floated away, on the jet stream, Daddy told us.

"I thought it would last longer," I said. "Will they do it again?"

Daddy laughed. "It's time to go home now and get some hot breakfast. Wasn't that amazing, kids?"

Everyone who had gotten up to watch the blast talked about it in school that day. "Did you see it?" Our desert land had been chosen once again for an important government project.

The front page of that night's newspaper had pictures of the before and after—frame houses before, no frame houses after, dummied soldiers before, no recognizable dummies after. Surprised cattle lay flat on their sides in the dead grass, their hair singed white on the up side. Yucca Flat. Frenchman Flat. Mercury Test Site. Household words.

"Nobody can get us now," my daddy said.

I don't think about it much, but sometimes when I punch my pillow and look for a cool spot to rest my cheek, ready to settle into sleep, the cloud mists into long airy fingers over everything, reaching across the stark blue.

Music in the Mojave

Sitting on the edge of the bed, I was dressed in baby doll pajamas. Elastic leg bands left red marks at the top of my thighs when I took them off, but that hadn't happened yet. I was feeling the morning cool from the wide-open window, rubbing the sleep from my eyes, and I was listening.

If I paid particular attention, I could almost hear the sun rising, the earth turning, the heat waves rising. I could imagine the subliminal buzz from the gigantic kachina doll towers erected in an endless line across the desert floor, their cables carrying electricity to southern California from Hoover Dam. In addition to that silent symphony, doors to my next-door neighbors' houses began opening and closing. Folded newspapers were tossed onto sidewalks. I could hear a swelling chorus of swamp coolers and their whirling blades, and, on top of all that, when I peered over the window's ledge, the sun orchestrated the rising colors of the hills and the distant pop-up mountains sprang to life. A crescendo like I had learned from Mrs. Bourne, my piano teacher. Music to my ears.

I needed to go to the bathroom but eyed the open window first, remembering Mother's reminder to close up everything before King Heat arrived to demand taxes. Before I made that final move to seize the day, however, I listened to the murmur of families: fathers starting car engines; mothers shouting, "Last call for breakfast"; voices floating from windows, my mother rattling the fry pan downstairs and someone setting the table. Reluctantly, I cranked the window until it jerked to a squeaky close. I pushed the handle down and locked it tight. Everything was much quieter then.

After breakfast, Mother instructed us. "Make your beds. Straighten your rooms. And don't forget you have to practice before you go out." My older sister, Elaine, took her turn first. I was next in line, then my brother, Steve—the pecking order. I made my bed and cleaned up while Elaine practiced, then took my turn on the piano bench. After I put in my time, I ran as fast as I could to the outside world, skipping, hopping, and skidding along the sidewalk in my new tennies. I listened for the squeaky sound of my shoes accompanied by the sound of high notes on a flute, one of the Widner kids practicing. Then there was the squawk: the sounds of a bauk-bauk-bauking chicken on a clarinet. More mothers. More music lessons. Music everywhere.

When I think back on it, those post-World War II mothers must have been hoping for something more than the Depression-tainted days they remembered, something more than bare-bones survival. They probably turned their pillows at night to find a cool spot to rest their cheeks. "Am I abandoning my daughters and sons to Red Rover, Kick the Can, and the ice cream truck?" In tangled sheets, they probably wondered what they could do to be a better mother.

My mother was one of them, I'm sure of that. She'd been raised on a farm in Idaho and had spent much time gazing out her window and wishing for something better. Maybe, in some way, her children could give her that wish. Maybe they could make a blue-ribbon badge for her and pin it on her blouse. This would let everyone know she was to be noticed for mothering outstanding, piano-playing, music-making children. That would give her credentials she never believed she had.

○

My mother wasn't chosen to take voice lessons. Her mother had chickens that laid eggs which, if sold, would make enough money to pay the vocal teacher for one student. This student happened to be her sister, Lois, and not my mother, Thora. Granted, there wasn't enough money to go around in those hard times that weren't even harder when the Depression hit because they were always tough, but I suspect my mother didn't like being passed over, basically being told she wasn't as good or didn't have the same potential. My mother probably never said anything to her mother, being the dutiful daughter and knowing the polite way to respond. Instead, she decided she wasn't good enough and that she didn't add up to more than one inch on that all-important ruler that measured diva possibility.

Sometimes she'd talk about herself and about how, when she was the young girl who looked out the upstairs windows longingly at the acres of farm fields dying because there wasn't enough water (even though a dam had been promised), she'd been marooned on a no-account farm without enough moisture to grow crops. Mama had nothing but a few school books to read, meals to prepare for the threshers who harvested what little had grown, kitchen floors to clean, and new straw to spread in the chicken coop. She must have dreamed larger dreams. Her father had been a successful farmer in another part of Idaho before the promise of Lost River and the offer he couldn't refuse. There were many pie-in-the-sky promises about what might have been, but Lost River, an appropriate name, was the place where the family tumbled into the abyss of disappointment.

After our mother married a man she met at the Agricultural College in Logan, Utah—one who was kind, who loved to dance, and who enlisted in the navy in World War II—she was transplanted to the Mojave Desert, an apt place for someone who'd watched no crops grow. Even so, she was always reminiscing about greener pastures. To make adjustments, she insisted on piano lessons and a daily regimen for all her children. When she sensed the curtain on her own aspirations closing, she must have envisioned us shining like stars on stage, the next best option. She yearned to have excellence, perfection, and culture flower in her living room, and we were the stones in her crown that she would polish.

○

When I came along and presented the possibility of a piano prodigy, my mother promised to do the dishes if I would play small vignettes from operas, the ones found in Volume 5 of the Scribner's red-colored, fake-leather, nine-book set, purchased from a door-to-door salesman. She would close her eyes and lift her voice, I swear, to some invisible someone out there who could hear how good she was. I listened and pretended not to. I loved hearing her sing when she abandoned her caring about who heard what. But, trouble was, whenever anyone shone the spotlight in her direction, she choked.

Once she tried to sing a solo at the church talent show. Clasping her hands, she stood in front of the burnished-orange curtains. While the accompanist played the introduction, I could see she was hesitant about starting. *Come on, Mother. I've heard you sing beautifully at home.* She began, shakily, and then started to anticipate the high notes. They were coming, like guerrillas or some such thing, and it was like she knew they would get her. She hesitated. Her throat closed up. I could hear tears in her voice. I bowed my head, wanting to shake it. *No, Mom. No. Stop. You can do this. Believe.* But she'd rehearsed the story too many times in her mind: her sister was better than she was; she shouldn't be trying; always a bridesmaid, never a bride kind of thing. She'd agreed at a cellular level that her mother knew more than she did about music.

Maybe, because of that, my mother wanted to show her mother she had something to contribute. "See. Look. Listen to my children play the piano. Talent comes out of my pores, too."

Being a dutiful daughter, I bought the whole thing, lock, stock, and barrel. "Yes, Mama. I'll do that for you. I'll grab the brass ring. I'll help you." Nothing was ever put into words. Nothing was ever said, but I started feeling anxious when asked to perform.

○

One can pound on a kettle with a stick of wood or on stretched skins, oil drums, tin cans, frying pans, or a drum set. There is a rhythm to the running of a river, to the coming in and going out of a wave, and even the heart has a beat. Music can happen by a pair of lips blowing air across the tops of bottles filled with different levels of water. It can be made by pushing air out of holes in pipes: a hornpipe, bagpipe, or didgeridoo. It can be made by a small wooden hammer striking or plucking a stretched-out string: a piano, a harpsichord, a clavichord; a bow crossing a string or fingers plucking. Kotos. Zithers. Dulcimers. There are a thousand-plus ways to make music, music, music.

I wish my mother could have believed in the music she'd been given. She didn't have faith in the simplicity of what she had or of what she'd been given. She always believed there was a pinnacle to reach, a higher culture, a more confident voice, something that would take her to a place other than what and where she was. Something, ironically, better than what the farmers in Idaho could attain, but I wonder if she ever heard the music of the desert.

○

Reality knocked the year Mother was asked to provide a costume for the piano recital. Mrs. Bourne, Boulder City's neighborhood teacher, was a sweet, kindly woman who lived two blocks from our home and taught piano lessons to provide extras for her own children. Mother was the proud owner of a Singer sewing machine on which she was determined to sew the clothes she couldn't afford. She worked late into the night assembling a costume that matched the title of one of the songs I'd learned— "Frosty the Snowman," the first of my two pieces I was to perform.

Mother tore, cut, stitched, and hemmed tired white sheets to create her vision of what Frosty the Snowman might look like. Bent over her sewing machine, she sewed elastic around the neck, the waist, and at the bottom to concoct two "almost" snowballs, but the bottom half of Frosty was too limp to look like much of a snowman. She got the brilliant idea of using a straightened-out clothes hanger, bending it into a circle, and stitching it to the middle of the bottom snowball. She sewed black buttons down the front, cut a stovepipe hat from black poster paper, and taped and re-taped it into a cylinder with a one-inch brim. With crumpled-up newspaper, lots of it, tons of it, she stuffed the costume until it was one big Frosty standing in our living room, me inside.

Mother re-stuffed me at the church, and I sat very precisely on the folding chair to keep my snowballs intact. But while I waited for my turn, the newspapers flattened, mashed, and became a general mess. All of this over the prim plaid dress my mother had sewn for the occasion. When it was showtime, I walked up the stairs to the stage, trying not to drop my innards onto the floor. I sat at the piano bench, the stiff wire hanger raising the snowball up to expose my dress and bare legs and interfere with my hands on the keyboard. What else could I do but reach around Frosty's distorted stomach and launch into his song?

"Thumpety thump thump." I sang the words to myself to

remember what came next. I must have been denying the awful reality of being on stage dressed in an old sheet, ready to tear it was so thin, newspaper dribbling out, but I played my piece with only one missed note. Undaunted, I launched into the Haydn "Sonatina," my fingers going faster than my mind, beating humiliation to the punch.

At the end of the recital, Mrs. Bourne awarded me with a plaster-of-Paris statuette of Beethoven for being "the most improved student." But it was only after listening to Mother berate herself for not thinking out the costume better than she had that I caught a whiff of how bad I must have looked. I embarrassed her and everyone else. It was *me* inside of that costume, not just a costume walking up on that stage by itself. I had let her down—my mother who hoped for more.

○

I didn't know much about Mrs. Ramsey, the new piano teacher Mother found in the hopes of new cultivation. Mrs. Ramsey was a cultured, precise, nice enough woman, married to an engineer for the Bureau of Reclamation, but her apartment smelled musty. Large, overstuffed armchairs, Persian rugs, its atmosphere sober compared to the wild bustling of three children and my pregnant mother in my own home. Our household was noisy and boisterous with nothing overstuffed in sight.

I breathed in a shallow way in Mrs. Ramsey's presence, but my mother had told me she was an excellent teacher. Her approach to the piano had a certain stiffness: scales, scales, and more scales; correct wrist position; arpeggios; Hanon exercises; learn the technique. Playing for Mrs. Ramsey, my fingers plodded across the blacks and whites. They slowly practiced a trill until it gained some speed. Piano became a discipline, and something inside of me was less sure about music and what it was or what it was supposed to be when I went to Mrs. Ramsey's.

The lessons didn't last much longer than a year before our

new baby sister was crawling and our father decided to move the family-busting-out-at-the-seams to Las Vegas and a yellow-stucco, two-story tract home at the edge of the desert. There were better business opportunities in that burgeoning town, he supposed, still small in 1954, even though our living room picture window exposed miles and miles of desert across the street, no other houses in sight, only whistling wind blowing sand into the window jambs.

Soon after settling in Las Vegas, Mother learned about Mrs. King, who would come to the house to give piano lessons. What a windfall, Mother must have imagined, at home without a car and with a new baby, still plagued with her yearning to have a child of hers fill that bruised hole in herself.

Mrs. King played at a cowboy bar on Boulder Highway on weekends. She dressed in blue jeans and blouses with cowgirl fringe on the pockets, then at other times in low-cut sundresses revealing a massively tired décolletage. She was about five feet tall with tightly curled gray hair while I, at age twelve, was already much taller. Mrs. King sometimes nodded off during the lessons while sitting on a dining room chair next to the piano. At other times she tapped her toe, though I imagined, with my newfound classical music superiority gleaned from Mrs. Ramsey, anybody who played at a cowboy bar was probably not the best teacher around.

But Mrs. King introduced me to "Bumble Bee Boogie," "Stardust," and "Malagueña," pieces with a beat and pieces I loved to play because people begged to hear them. The relatives would say "wow" when my father requested I "play something they'll like." I felt some kind of power swelling up inside that I could make music to please and catch such attention. Ordinarily, the aunts and uncles kept talking, but this time with this music, they clapped their hands and said, "Bravo. Hey, you're really something."

Nothing made sense anymore.

○

When I entered high school, I received a telephone call from Christina DeVore, a classical ballet teacher in Las Vegas, the wife of a columnist for the *Las Vegas Review Journal*. She said Mrs. King had mentioned my name and would I be interested in coming to the studio for an audition. She needed an accompanist for her ballet classes. On the lookout for extra cash, usually earned by babysitting next door, I said yes, I'd come by. My mother even liked the idea.

I auditioned; I passed muster; I began playing for classes two afternoons a week after school. I was given a book with excerpts from famous ballets—*Giselle, Rosamunde, Swan Lake,* and *Coppélia*—and short, rhythmic snippets of famous pieces of music that kept the ballerinas leaping and twirling. I learned to keep a strict, never-faltering beat with the help of Christina's snapping fingers. Introduced to the world of pliés, rond de jambes, fouettés, and pas de boureés, I met the young ballerinas. I met their parents, some of them wives of hotel orchestra conductors, who sat and watched from the same alcove where I and the piano sat.

Rotating my eyes to their corners, I devoured the sight of the dancers twirling, then leaping, their split legs suspended in the air. I wanted to lift into such a magical moment. This was what I'd been looking for, this was what I wanted, not tired, confusing, old piano lessons. That must have shown on my face. One day, Christina invited me to join a beginning class. This I did for a few lessons before Mother reminded me that my piano came first and that my time was too limited to accomplish all and everything. "Big eyes and small stomachs," she said. Then, one day after class, Christina suggested I might study piano with Mr. Schmidt.

"You have talent," she said. "He could take your playing to a new level." Louis Basil, the father of the prima ballerina in the studio and also the leader of the house band at the Sahara Hotel, was waiting for his daughter to change clothes. He overheard our conversation. "Good idea," he chimed in. "You do have promising talent, young lady."

Thus encouraged, I showed up at Mr. Schmidt's address in the heart of downtown Las Vegas. The minute I glimpsed the interior of his small home, however, I felt the big wilt happen inside of me, the big melt, the memory of Frosty dropping paper innards on the stage floor. This man and his studio were Mrs. Ramsey and her apartment magnified twenty-fold. Hundreds of scores were piled high on the lid of his grand piano. Shelves of gold-embossed, real-leather-bound books dominated the wood-paneled room. When I heard him speak, I suspected an Austrian accent, though little did I know who sounded like what except from World War II movies.

Mr. Schmidt asked me to play something, and I froze. My fingers stalled, balked, and performed all manner of maneuvers reserved for frostbite. Every pore of my body seemed an ice cube. I couldn't show off for Mr. Schmidt. Not in a million tries. Mr. Schmidt became witness to the fact that, before his eyes, sat a fraud.

"It's all right," he said several times and patted my shoulder. "Try again."

I'll never know how, but I managed to eke out a few decent measures of a Beethoven sonata, good enough that Mr. Schmidt invited me to take lessons from him. He was kind, caring, even a gentleman. But in my nervous frenzy, all I could think was, "Run." I made excuses about why lessons wouldn't work right now and almost ran out the door to where my mother waited in the car, hoping for good results. "I'm just a poseur," I said to her after slamming the car door. She frowned. "What are you talking about?"

○

After my brief encounter with Mr. Schmidt, I dropped piano studies, much to my mother's chagrin. "Enough is enough," I told her. "How good do I need to be and where am I going with this? Music is in my bones. Why do I need to study something that's bigger than studies?"

When I auditioned for a different opportunity, both in my freshman and sophomore years, it was finally announced that I had been chosen to be a Las Vegas Rhythmette, a member of a marching, precision-dancing group of high school girls—one of the supreme things I wanted at the time. This was something more than piano practicing, for sure, maybe because people had been calling me Bones and Skinny Minny. Even though my mother cast an aspersive eye on the Rhythmettes, telling me to be patient for the truly good things of life, I was determined to be more than that: voluptuous, sexy, alluring like the pictures of showgirls in the newspapers, the ones poised on diving boards or sitting cross-legged in deck chairs. No doubt, puberty was competing with any study of music I'd ever known. I wanted to show off for real. I wanted to move, dance, kick my legs higher than high, and wear Rhythmette costumes with their short skirts that displayed my long legs, which were looking good—better than the rest of rail-thin me. I still performed my razzle-dazzle piano pieces for school assemblies ("Malagueña" and "Bumble Bee Boogie") and accompanied various musicians at church and school as well as the Choralettes of Las Vegas High School. But I always had the feeling I was a hoax. A showboat, not much more. Not a real musician—the kind who cared about mastery. Dine and dash. That was me.

After my senior year at Las Vegas High School, I enrolled at Brigham Young University as a political science major, thinking I would meet the men who were going into politics. I also won the office of freshman class secretary. I could make a difference in the swirl of males commandeering the world. I was a woman on the move. But something else called to me. Genetics. Hormones. The music of the heavens, whatever it was. Push. Pull. I married after my junior year, barely turned twenty-one, thinking I was getting old. We moved to Palo Alto where my new husband attended Stanford Law School. After working one year in the development office, luckily, I made my declaration. "I need to finish my degree. No ifs, ands, or buts." Gratefully, my husband agreed. He could identify with my growing sense of uselessness in our little cottage on a Los Altos Hills estate where I did secretarial work and trimmed the roses in the rose garden to pay the rent. But he insisted I pursue my education in something more natural and integral to my life than political science. "Like piano," he said. "Music."

At San Jose State (I didn't bother applying to Stanford—too much money for tuition and I didn't believe I was good enough, of course), I realized it was time to stop kidding myself, basically. I'd finished all of my general requirements at BYU, so was free to face the hard work I'd been reluctant to do with Mr. Schmidt, that I'd been reluctant to do all along. I practiced four to five hours a day, two measures at a time, hands alone, all the time keeping the tempo set by a metronome.

I received my degree in piano performance and also gave birth to two sons—one born with hemophilia (wherever that came from I'll never know), the other born in an astoundingly short time after the other, though I didn't think that would deter my newfound music career. I'd fit it all in somehow. We moved to Salt Lake City, where I immediately signed on with a professor who'd studied at a Paris conservatory. This appealed to my elitist ambitions and to the suppressed longing I must have inherited. While my sons slept, I concentrated. I practiced. I coaxed the piano keys to speak of whatever was being asked by the composer. I could do this. I would do this. I bragged to my mother. "I'm studying Chopin. The nocturnes. The ballades. Brahms." I showed off when we visited my parents. "Your technique," my mother would beam. I was an official student of music with confidence I'd never had. I would become a concert pianist. I would. I could, if I worked hard enough. Work harder. Work even harder. Concentrate. Believe. Work harder than hard. Concert-level precision. Perfection.

But then my oldest son, a three-year-old, died of a cerebral hemorrhage—the hemophiliac whose blood would not stop running. Run away, blood. Run where you will. Hemorrhage. Bleed out. All of a sudden, Geoffrey was gone. Not there to kiss on the top of his head or to read stories or sing lullabies to. My beautiful baby. My brief encounter with his life. Slipped away.

Not as much mattered after that. Music, which had always been my go-to, my path to salvation as outlined by my mother, morphed into a strange bedfellow. It became a struggle between listening to the glorious music I could hear through my wide-open window as opposed to the dogged climb to technique—perfectly educated and executed. I didn't like what it had become for me: technique, doggedness, repetition, perfection vs. the joy of music, music, music. Where was the joy?

I terminated serious piano study after that but never stopped playing the piano. I played lunch and dinner music at a Scottish restaurant in Salt Lake City. I played the keys of a black-lacquered grand piano at a nightclub, wearing rhine-stones on my collar and cuffs. A professional musician, no less. But I still wondered. Perfection was so far in the distance, so beyond my fingertips. And yet it felt all mixed up. What about pure music? The music that happened in the spheres, in the des-ert, in the blank spaces?

My limited perception of what it takes to produce music was skewed, even twisted by what I thought teachers and my mother expected. This was not to say I didn't love a well-performed concerto or symphony. I could still swoon over someone else's performance, especially when their music surfaced through the cracks. But I remember the mornings in the Mojave. Something bigger was outside my window. I didn't need to be a mindless slave chained to a repetitive fear of less-than-perfect. What was perfection anyway?

I had become my mother—wanting to make the most beautiful music but somehow not good enough to do so. My inheritance from her longing was that I was never good enough, never just a child of music and the sounds I could make with the piano or the simplicity of my voice. I had to be better to be good enough, but I never reached "good enough," not ever. I always felt a restlessness to go to the next level, but when I'd get there, I had to go a step further. I wish my mother and I wouldn't have thought so much about how we sounded, about how we were being received, or about whether or not any of our mothers thought we were good enough. I wish we could have flirted with the audience. Winked one eye. Taken them on. "I'm up here and you're out there. Let's go for it." I wish we could have bartered with and teased them, instead of being so worried about measuring up to some unreachable standard.

Sometimes my thoughts return to the desert in the morning and the stars in the sky on a summer night. I wonder if all those mothers and fathers who wanted music for their children were urged on by the sound of heat rising up in the morning and settling down at night, or by the rhythm of the moon and its phases. In the end, music is not about us, the aspiring virtuosi who secretly and not so secretly wish to impress and astound and reach beyond ourselves. It happens above and beyond the training, the practice, the study. Once in a while, it transcends itself and touches the elemental, the supreme, and ascends to a place which no one can describe with words. It's a conduit to something else, maybe something as grand as the Pacific Ocean, the Grand Canyon, the Himalayas, and maybe even the Mojave Desert on a summer morning.

MT. CHARLESTON ON MY MIND

Desert creatures, all of us in those days, escaping to the mountain for the day—a reminder that there was other terrain besides the Mojave and other landscapes besides long, flat, rolling stretches of what most would call wasteland. Las Vegas was a small town when I was eleven, before the Strip was much at all. The chamber of commerce was trying to get some respect but their poster child was considered by most to be a dusty outpost. So, there we were—off to higher altitude to cool down, to hike, to shout into the thin, clear air as if we were hunters and trappers from the Olden Days or yodelers from the Swiss Alps. Everybody was dressed in an assortment of Davy Crockett hats, stout shoes, padded socks, and long pants to protect their legs from the branches of scraggly trees and bugs that might bite.

Enclosed in a green Plymouth, early fifties vintage and a bit of a box, my family was in a caravan of cars driving to Mt. Charleston—fifty miles from Las Vegas—for a church picnic: the Fifth Ward of the Church of Jesus Christ of Latter-day Saints. It was a friendly, prayerful, cheerful group who believed they were ordained by God to pursue the wholesome lives they'd chosen. Fluffy clouds frolicked in the most-always-blue sky. What a grand day to be in the mountains.

On the narrow road that wound up and up, our mother asked our dad to pull over for a minute. "Let's see if the pine nuts are ready yet. We'll catch up to the others." We—my older sister, Elaine, and younger brother, Steve—added our loud approval of that idea. We were eager to check out the harvesting possibilities of the piñon tree nuts, come back as soon as possible, lay a sheet beneath the pines, shake the branches, and let the ripe ones fall onto our trap. We'd tie them in a hobo's bundle and toss our booty into the trunk of our car. At home, we'd bake them in the oven, slow, two hundred degrees for two hours, then crack them open, ever so carefully. They were the tiniest of nuts, and we didn't want to obliterate them with our digging fingernails. Such a lot of work for a mini-bite, but such a satisfying one. Worth the trouble in those days.

Each of us tumbled out of the car in anticipation, not caring about whether the nuts were big or small because we could smell those pines. We ran to the dusty branches and examined the progress of that year's crop, touching the yellow tar oozing out of the cracks in the tree trunk, tempted to chew the tar, though we'd been told not to. Bugs, maybe? "Two more weeks," Mother said, and then we all returned to the car with that smell on our hands and fingers and the cuffs of our long-sleeved shirts. Nothing was better than that piney smell and fresh mountain air.

Once we settled back in the car, Mother fed Baby Kathy a bottle, then rearranged the baby on her shoulder and patted her back, coaxing a gaseous burp out of that miniature body.

"Cute baby," I must have said because Baby Kathy was, indeed, a cute baby whom we all thought was a supreme prize. I reached up to the front seat, patted Kathy's wispy hair, and said "Oooooo" with squeezed, kissing lips. We called this response a Buzzzh, which usually included a pinch of someone's cheek. A family habit.

Dad was now driving the car on the Mt. Charleston road, minus the cars we'd come up with. We'd catch up soon or, if not, we'd meet at the designated picnic spot. We knew the destination. I could still smell the piñon pines out the open car window, the pine tar on my fingers, the wind blowing my hair to some exotic wig style. We were in the wilds and free. And we were all together—our family, which we loved beyond anything else.

We never did catch up with the caravan but after driving for twenty minutes more to get to the picnic site, we unloaded our bags of food, our cooler, our extra jackets, and then sprinted to get in line for our annual hike on the Mt. Charleston Trail, which most of us never finished. We were always excited and ready to conquer the peak (or the end of the trail, who even knew?) every single time. We'd tried two or three times to climb to the top but hadn't made it yet. We were children: "Dad, I'm tired. I can't go on. I'll die if I take another step."

Mom stayed behind with the baby, and we set out for the grand adventure with a brave group of hikers. But before long, the trail seemed never-ending, impossible, larger than the largest challenge in life, steeper than steep, and, of course, we youngsters moaned loudly enough that our dad finally gave in. (I don't remember who made it to the top or if anyone did.) We returned to the bottom, carefully, carefully, so as not to trip over bared roots or slide on worn, hardened dirt that had seen the soles of too many hikers' boots and sort-of hikers' shoes. But none of us noticed that the canopy of trees was hiding the heavens. Massive clouds were pushing against each other, vying for the title of King of the Sky. I don't remember much of this, however, being that I was so busy watching for loose rocks and the bottom of the trail.

When we got back, I rummaged through the green Coleman cooler and saw that we'd brought a dessert, some homemade root beer, and some baby bottles. Mother had arranged plates on a picnic table on a colorful tablecloth while Kathy slept on the back seat of our car, pillows stuffed in the place where we usually kept our feet so she wouldn't roll over and fall into the pit. We were ravenous and ready to eat after the hike. The organizers of the outing had brought wieners and buns for a wienie roast, and everyone who'd come to the picnic had brought a dessert to share—a 9 x 13 pan of brownies, still in the pan; an apple pie; a sheet cake covered with slathery frosting made of Crisco, the staple shortening of the day. S'mores, too. We'd brought Rice Krispy treats made of melted marshmallows, butter, and Rice Krispies. Cruncha, cruncha, Krispies sticking to my teeth and playing havoc with my new braces.

We drank Hawaiian punch brought in a tall drink cooler, selected paper napkins kept under a rock so they wouldn't blow away, and ate with regular knives and forks, which we'd take home and wash after we used them. There were games, too: three-legged races and potato-sack races. Everyone screamed and laughed while clouds gathered overhead, shadowing the sun, covering it up while we hopped and jumped and ran from one end of the campsite to the other.

At the end of the festivities on that particular day in Mt. Charleston, Brother Pulsipher said our closing prayer. He asked that all of us would return to Las Vegas in safety, that our caravan would make it back to our homes with no troubles, that God would watch over us and bless us. Each and every one. I'd heard that kind of prayer at least a hundred times, if not more, and tapped my shoe until he was finished and pushed my elbow into my friend Leslie's side to see if she could stay in balance with her eyes closed. She elbowed me back, but then we decided to make a show of reverence, at least for the amen.

When we got ready to pack the car, the overhead clouds had grown unusually ominous—steel gray, the blackest gray one could imagine. They seemed to be putting up their dukes to fight each other. There was cracking of lightning and thunder, louder than the F-15 jets from Nellis Air Force Base that flew overhead and broke the sound barrier. The rain began slowly at first, giving us time to finish packing our car before we got too soaked. But just after we'd jumped inside, slammed the doors, and after our father started the engine and crept the Plymouth down the road that was becoming super wet, the sky opened and poured water as if from a celestial bucket. The rain sheeted onto the roof of our car in brutal, thunking drops—the heaviest I'd ever heard, a colossal dumping of water that made our car sound like a tin drum with a drummer whose sticks had gone berserk. We looked over our shoulders and, because we had pulled out first, saw the headlights of the cars behind us—jittery bubbles of light in the cloudburst.

I felt very small and insecure but thought Steve might feel smaller and more insecure. I took hold of his twig-like arm. "You okay?" I asked. He was wide-eyed and nervous, too. We could barely see out of the windows of our car, and our windshield wipers couldn't keep up with the pounding rain. Dad kept driving, slowly, his mouth open because he couldn't swallow his amazement. He tried to negotiate the road through blurry windows. It was like we were beneath a waterfall or, even more than that, totally underwater. Our baby sister was crying, and the rest of us were too stunned to cry because that storm was so overpowering and bigger than the biggest storm ever.

Suddenly, as if someone stronger than was humanly possible had been aiming right at us, we felt a huge thump on the back of our car. Huger than huge. The car jerked to the right then swerved to the left, tires squealing. Daddy held onto the steering wheel with both hands, gripping them tighter than tight, his face white and panicked.

"Daddy," a couple of us screamed as the car screeched to a halt.

In a flash, Elaine, Steve, and I switched around in our seats, leaned our chins against the top of the back cushions, hip-to-hip on our knees, and looked for the headlights behind us, which had disappeared. There was a gigantic river of rocks sliding across the road. Where was the rest of our group? Red mud, boulders, and one gigantic boulder bigger than our car were now sitting in the middle of the road where we were one second before, surrounded by a running river of more red mud, small rocks. It looked as if the whole side of the hill had crumbled onto the highway. The road was no longer a road but a raging watercourse with a humongous boulder sitting in the middle. And now, for a fleeting minute, we were sitting in the middle of the river, which flowed as high as our doors. Luckily, our car still ran when Daddy turned the key in the ignition, restarted the car, and drove further down the road out of harm's way. Then we stopped again—all of us wanting to know what had happened to the rest of our group.

After we were sure that the river was not running after us or spilling over the high side of the road anymore, Dad spoke. "We could have been killed," he whispered very quietly to our mother. His voice was shaky. Our dad. Even though all I could see was his profile, I'd never seen his face looking that white. "Did you see the size of that boulder?" he asked.

"I can't believe how close we came . . ." My mother's voice was shaky, too, almost too soft for words to be formed, almost a whisper in the stillness of the aftershock.

"That boulder was almost bigger than our car. It was like a bomb hit us."

"I can't stop shaking," Mother said. "Look at my hands. Kathy. Baby. Shhh. Stop crying. Oh, heaven's above, we were almost . . ."

"I better get out and check what's happened to the people behind us. All I can say is that somebody was watching over us," my dad said as he opened the door. "One second. I wonder how long that is in divine time? It's hardly raining now."

These words made me want to fold my arms and say a prayer of gratitude but all I could think about was that one second and my daddy out there in all the mud. If we'd taken one tiny, little second longer to say goodbye to our friends, we would have been crushed beneath that house-sized boulder that now sat on the road to Mt. Charleston. The thought crowded all other thoughts out of my mind, and we three kids in the back seat had nothing to say—unusual for us. We peered out the window at the rain still falling, gently now, and wondered what Daddy would find out about the others behind us. Did anyone get buried? Would the rest ever be able to get through? Could someone clear this road? Had we done something wrong for this to happen? Was this a warning?

"Everybody's safe on the other side," my dad said as he hopped back into the front seat, his face no longer white. "We'll go alert the park rangers. Find somebody to get this road cleared."

We'd made it to the other side, the downhill side. The rest of the cars seemed okay on the other side, and the road would be cleared as soon as moving equipment could be found, the ranger said.

○

I could say that God was protecting us. I still believe. The idea of God is how I was taught when I was learning how to walk, when I wore Mary Janes and ankle socks, when I sprouted pimples and wore glasses. Even when I was fifteen and sang, "I am a child of God, and He has sent me here. Has given me an earthly home, with parents, oh so dear." But how can we possibly understand the thinking of the immortal?

If God protects some people, then why doesn't He (the pronoun I was taught and still use) protect all of the people? Why are some chosen to be saved and some not? People might be denied entry to an airplane at the last minute, for instance. They can be frustrated beyond the beyond yet tell everyone they were saved by God when the plane crashes and kills everyone aboard the plane they missed boarding. But what about all of those who perish? What is the fairness of that equation? What about earth-quakes or people who are blown away or crushed in hurricanes? People who forget to fasten their seatbelts in automobile accidents or those washed away in tsunamis bigger than the towns they live in? Those caught in a pandemic with the coronavirus wrestling people into the grave?

I have heard God blamed when bad things happen and yet praised when "good" happens. But is there a someone who decides when life has been lived long enough? Or short enough? An even more esoteric question might be: Is life so valuable anyway, or is it a mere passage of time, unremarkable in the eternal perspective, a blip on the continuum?

If we would have been one second, one eternal moment, longer in coming down from Mt. Charleston, then we would have been buried beneath that massive rock that rolled to the middle of the road and that later had to be moved by bulldozers. Split seconds. Good luck, fortunate timing, or God's beneficence? The other cars had slowed down in the chaos of rain, thank the heavens for their slow descent, but our car was one second ahead of the mud, the shit-colored water, the destruction and chaos. We could have been buried there. Smashed. All six of us—mother, father, Elaine, Steve, Kathy, and me: our family that was all-important to each of us. But why were we separated from the others? Why did they have to wait? And what would have happened if we or they died? Would we have known we were dead? Would we have been eulogized? What would people have said at our funerals? That it was our time to go? That we had lived honorable lives and would be blessed accordingly? Is there a heaven where we would all go and be together and laugh and joke and smell the scent of pine nuts?

But we have lived. I have to remember that, I do. And people told us we were blessed by God that day.

I want to say that I know someone listens to our prayers, to our pleas, to our yearnings, that there is a personal God who listens to our very heartbeats. But people who offer the same prayers sometimes go down with the airplane when it crashes.

Maybe Brother Pulsipher's prayer saved us. It makes me breathe easier to say we were blessed that day, riding down the mountain, singing some feel-good song about Jesus loving us, and a boulder crashing into our bumper—leaving a massive dent and letting us know how close we came. I feel better when I think the finger of God nudged us a bit faster down the mountain, good and loyal Saints that we were.

Love Via Johnny

Johnny Mathis's velvet voice drifts through the living room, his words more powerful than the sound of the air conditioner. Don't get me wrong. I'm grateful for the cool air. We live in a desert after all. It's still hot outside, even though the sun's gone down. In fact, it's super hot. I don't understand why the nights are almost more sweltering than the days. It should cool off when the sun goes down, but there's barely relief in the summer— maybe not until the early hours of morning. So, I repeat, thank goodness for air conditioning. Luckily, we're wearing shorts and tank tops and lying on the shag carpet in Cheryl's living room listening to music. We'll stay cool enough.

Except, my mind is wandering. These nights are sensual. The sun has gone down, the stars are out. It's almost like a person can reach out with her fingertips and feel the velvet of night. Stroke it. Put it next to her face. Caress it. Bunch it up into wrinkled silk. Maybe I'm thinking about lying under the cover of night. Under a sheet. With someone.

"Chances are, 'cause I wear a silly grin the moment you come into view, chances are you think that I'm in love with you." Ah

love. I sigh. Wouldn't it be nice? Love is the thing I've been hoping would show up for years, at least since I was twelve. Johnny's
voice floats just like he must have done when he soared over the
bar as a high jumper in high school. He was even an Olympic
hopeful, but now he's singing to me and Cheryl. "Chances Are."
*"Just because my composure sort of slips, the moment that your
lips meet mine . . ."*

We'll be going back to Las Vegas High School in a few weeks.
We'll be seniors—the class of '61. Maybe someone will be waiting to fall in love with me, someone who can really see who I am.
This hope, this possibility for love, is playing on Cheryl's hi-fi,
on the 45 rpm we play over and over. Sometimes I think I'd be
flattered by anyone who wore long pants taking notice, though
that's not what I've been taught, that's not what I really think.
One must be choosy. Look for the best, for the most compatible.
A good man. But after listening to Johnny, I'm full of wanting—
wanting someone to come along and see me hidden behind my
nervousness and shyness and gangly self that doesn't seem to fold
in the right directions. I've tried to hide between hunched shoulders, behind a timid, almost neurotic laugh. Sometimes, I curse
myself for being what seems mousy and insignificant, though
that's harsh. Still, I wish I were more flirty, edgy, and careless,
meaning I wish I didn't care so much. The Purple Streak. The
Bomb. The Flippant One.

Cheryl's parents are gone for the evening, and though I don't
tell her, I want to bury myself in the shag of her carpet. Cover
myself with the strands of thread. Disappear in the warp and weft
as if we could all merge into oneness, wholeness, into love. She's
lying on her stomach, leaning on her elbows, raising her legs
behind her knees. Sometimes she puts her heels together. Sometimes she switches one leg above the other. She's got a boyfriend.
I bet she's thinking about him, forget the chances out there. It's
not fair that she has someone and I don't, but she's my friend and
she's pretty. Short and compact. Curvy. I'm a tall drink of water,

straight as a board mostly. I'm starting to fill out a little though, and I'm hoping there are curves ahead.

But Johnny. Something about his voice makes love seem like the only thing anyone could want. I think I need someone to love me. Me above all others. I do. But if I love anybody too obviously or am too needy, they don't love me back. It's happened before. Maybe the popular boys—those cool representatives of the high school state-of-mind—are embarrassed to be seen with Skinny Minny—tall, thin me. I'm not exactly eye candy, I know that. Sexy is not a word I'd apply to myself. But I keep hoping. I'm becoming, after all. I'm getting the things I need—bumps for breasts and curves, slowly but surely, and I have my period.

Last spring, I told another friend that I wanted to ask Bruce to the Girls' Reverse Dance. She did me the big favor of warning him. She did. What a traitor. Because she had prepared him for the shock of me asking him, he was prepared to say "no, thank you." He said "no" very quickly, almost before I finished asking him, and that "no" still rides high in my memory. How could a friend betray me like that? Bruce told me "no" out there in the stark sunshine with a totally blinding blue sky. I'll never undo that hurt, even if I understand practical explanations. Maybe he'd rather go with someone else. Someone sexy. Like my friend, maybe—the one who told him that someone unworthy was about to ask him to the dance. She was a viper is all I can say.

"Chances are, you think my heart's your Valentine."

I need someone to come along and take notice. Not only that, but someone who desires me, someone who calls me at night and tells me he can't wait to see me again. I could ride next to him in his car and shoulders could touch. We'd go to Sill's Drive-In and cruise past the flashing neon bulbs dotting the roof line. We'd listen to the sounds of radios blaring from every car. People would ask, "Are they going together?" And I'd smile to myself, fingering the engraved silver disc on the chain around my neck—the one with my love's name in cursive.

"*Just because,*" I sing along, "*my composure sort of slips.*" My composure won't slip and slide when that certain someone sees me walking down the hall at high school next fall. I'm ready. I'll be someone who's arrived at sweet womanness. A blossom. Someone more than ready.

With the shag next to my face, though not quite long enough to reach my mouth, thank goodness, I really wouldn't want to gag on a shag rug, I think about Josh. That's what I'll call him. He was that one boy who telephoned me when I was a sophomore. Over the phone, he read excerpts from a sex book about positions and possibilities. Is this really happening? I wondered as he read. If someone were to ask, I'd say he was horny and touched in the head because it seemed that sex was all he could think about. But I listened, I grant you that, more attentively than I imagined I could listen. My hormones were as busy as his testosterone, both of us in perilous puberty, while my mother did dishes in the next room.

Maybe he wasn't all that different from me. Maybe we were both controlled by the Big Urge to procreate. Being a boy, he couldn't help himself, at least that's what I've been told about teenage boys: all they can think about is sex. Forget about love. Yet, I felt so shocked. Look at all the people walking around, created and born in the same way. Some of the way-overweight and some of the plainest women at my church still amaze me that they have children. I can't visualize them doing "it," though I guess nobody escapes that process if he or she has children. Josh was probably trying to reach across that chasm between boys and girls to find the place he could connect, even if he had to use words and explanations of pictures to bridge the gap between us, to somehow create his dream-time phallus, longer than long, wistfully seeking a home, a place to be caressed and held.

Once, he told me about the time he was slow dancing with a girl at a Friday-night-after-the-game dance, how he got a hard-on and had to put his hand over his crotch when he walked her back to sit down. I couldn't help but wonder how much she noticed or whether he had to hurry to the bathroom to straighten everything out or not. How would that be to be busted so visibly? To have your craving for sex so apparent? And, hardest of all for me to understand, it's out of his control, that thing called a penis that has its own say in the way it rises and falls. It's no Roman Empire with a definite beginning and end. No sense of history, except predictability.

I listened to Josh read and tell me those things, curious though I pretended not to be. I was horny, too, wanting someone to touch me and tell me I was beautiful and appealing and all things magical. But I listened with divided attention as he plunged deeper into the text about the rawest of sex—almost as if it was happening for real. I could get in trouble for being interested. A teacher at church had told us that fornication or adultery was next to murder. A Big Sin, one of the biggest of all, and we girls should be on the watch for any slide toward the breaking or bending of that rule. That warning probably saved me when Josh and I went on our one and only date and saw *Around the World in 80 Days* at a drive-in theater. His hands started to explore, and part of me allowed myself to fantasize what it would feel like to have someone's hands on my flesh. No one's hands had touched my flesh before, except when I was a baby with diapers and baths, of course. But I told him to keep them to himself. He wasn't the man of my dreams to begin with. But what if he had been? Would I have responded differently to someone else? I wonder if Cheryl and her boyfriend talk about these things.

Oh, Johnny. It's all so complicated—people wanting to be loved, to be held, to be stroked, or whatever they need to be. But you make it sound so right, so desirable, so possible. How could anyone sing the way you do and make all of us wish we could be right there, listening to you, taking the chance of being in love?

Why do you have that kind of voice—so finely pitched, so sensual, so vivid about what it means to be in love?

"Let's go to Sill's," Cheryl says as the phonograph record reaches the place where it has no sound except a repetitive thunk against a final, single thread stamped into the plastic. The needle needs to be picked up and started again, but then, it's time to do something else. And we both know what that will be.

I stretch out, pointing my toes, extending my arms, straightening my elbows, and saying "ahhh." She's probably hoping she'll meet up with her boyfriend, that he'll be back from the Tracks where the boys drink beer before they look for the girls who inspire the hope that they'll get what they want. I don't know what Cheryl does when she gets in the car with the one she loves, nor do I think much about it. *It's not for me to say*, I sing to myself, and then laugh because I've snitched a line from Johnny. How he haunts my life. I hum the rest of that melody, hoping that tonight we'll have happy hunting.

"Okay," I say, pushing up from the shag carpet, pulling my car keys out of my pocket, jangling them as if they belong to me. I re-tuck my shirt, check my lipstick to see if I still have some on my lips, and straighten the mussed hair at the back of my head. Cheryl turns out the lights. We lock the door behind us.

When we drive to Sill's in my parents' unsexy Plymouth, which they let me borrow for the evening, we look at the parked cars lined up in the stalls. Some are full of girls, some with boys slouched down in their seats nursing a beer. Some are being served by carhops, and some are drinking Cokes out of straws. I wonder if that someone I'm looking for might be here, in one of these cars, waiting for me.

Cheryl's boyfriend's not driven into Sill's yet, and I wonder if the one I'm looking for is with him out at that bridge in the desert where the tracks cross a gully, shored up by crossbars of heavy wood: the Tracks. I've never been there but I can only imagine what it's like. Is my someone with the boys tonight?

Are they thinking about "Chances Are" or composure sort of slipping or is that only me wishing and wishing on stars that are twinkling overhead but oh so far away? Is he on his way to the drive-in, looking for someone just like me? Oh, please, be somewhere. He has to be somewhere. A good boy? A bad boy? A dangerous man-to-be in one of these cars? Anxiously opening the door when he sees us drive through in the Plymouth, which has suddenly become a Magic-Mobile with stardust on its fenders. Holding up his hand, saying, "Wait."

Johnny's on the radio now, crooning again. "*Wonderful, wonderful.*" Johnny who makes all the world seem silvery, like glistening thread on a spool where regular thread is supposed to be. He's a man who lives in the magic of moonlight that could shower down on us at any moment if we're only patient enough, though, who wants to be patient?

And we cruise.

ODE TO THE MOJAVE

O

—/M\—

"About thirty thousand years ago, at the close of the Pleistocene or ice age, this region we call southern Nevada, now so barren, was green and well-watered. . . . That was the day of generous summer showers and winter snows, of forests and lush grassy meadows. . . . Many of the creatures then alive would look strange to us today; the mammoth or American elephant, queer native horses and camels, large and small; giant buffalo with horns six feet across, and most curious of all, lumbering stupid ground-sloths, looking like imbecile, long-tailed bears. . . . So southern Nevada's first man found it when he came, probably drifting in small bands from the north where their forebearers had crossed to Alaska from Siberia."

—Arabell Lee Hafner, *100 Years on the Muddy*

One

Call me whatever you want. The year is 2007, I'm riding my bicycle on a narrow road asphalted on top of a desert, and I'm thinking that names don't matter, not really. This landscape reminds me that names eventually blow away. Maybe they matter as a point of reference for Hawaiians, Caucasians,

Pakistanis, or Peruvians. But I wonder. Does a grain of sand have a name? Or a drop of water? Then why human beings? There are lots of us around. Now. Then. Arriving. Departing.

I'll ignore the desert's wisdom and tell you my name anyway. However, I warn you, I'm ubiquitous. Hard to pin down. You can call me my given name. Or Chloe Annalisa. Or Moapat Woman-Who-Never-Gives-Her-Sacred-Name-Away. All I can say is that I feel like only one of a zillion people who've inhabited this planet, perhaps many times. Does a name matter in the stretch of eons? And is there such a thing as one name forever, imprinted in the Book of Time?

I approach the boundaries of the Lake Mead National Recreation Area—a dull name for a bizarre landscape. The ranger station that charges an entry fee is about two, maybe three minutes away. My bike inches toward this small brown building and this ranger-on-duty in the high Mojave Desert east of Las Vegas. A land always short on water, but the word *short* is too generous.

Twenty miles back, I left my car at the side of the almost-deserted road, took my bike off the rack, and set out on the day trip I've been planning for a year, way before this morning when a woman working in the Lost City Museum in Overton told me that a few years back, in 2005 and for the first time since 1938, the water in Lake Mead sank low enough for St. Thomas to be visible. I live four hundred miles north of here in the Rocky Mountains and have always been curious to know where that town was built. I had no clue it would be visible. St. Thomas was a town named after Thomas S. Smith, the appointed leader of the Mormon pioneer settlement built at the confluence of the Virgin and Muddy Rivers in 1865, abandoned in 1871, later resettled only to be buried beneath the artificial Lake Mead in 1938.

The ranger in her deep-dark-nature-green ranger hat waves me through without collection since I'm on a bicycle and the clouds overhead are threatening to pop any time now. "Maybe you should wait until another day," she says when I tell her where I'm going.

"I don't have that luxury," I say, then pedal off. Uphill.

Two

In this life, this now, this me mostly known by the name I was given by my parents, I lived in this desert as a child in Boulder City, Nevada, fifty miles south of here. Even then, I suspected Nature didn't ask for Hoover Dam to capture and enslave the waters of the Colorado River, though most everyone was proud of this gigantic feat. The engineers and the politicians built the dam to last forever. They created a colossal lake. But now, even though the dam will probably last into infinity, what about the water?

Sitting astride a bicycle seat and pedaling hard up yet another hill, I can see that Lake Mead, where people swim, boat, water ski, and fish, is low—the lowest I have ever seen it. Bathtub rings circle the shore and the bottom of one intake tower almost doesn't reach the water. I wonder how much longer it can last, if its water will evaporate into a Lake Mead of the sky.

The Rocky Mountains dictate the amount of water in the Colorado River, which crosses seven large states: Colorado, Wyoming, New Mexico (the Upper Basin), and Utah, Nevada, Arizona, and California (the Lower Basin), not to mention Mexico at the delta next to the Pacific—an entity often ignored by the states and their claims on water.

Year after year, the Rockies are expected to deliver on the promises made to those along the river's banks and to the cities of Las Vegas, Phoenix, and Los Angeles. But the lawmakers have allocated more water than the river has to give. The mountains follow a different timetable, one not drafted by construction workers, public minds, and engineers.

Three

In 1952, I sat on the back seat of the family car descending the hill from Boulder City on the way to Lake Mead. To a nine-year-old, the lake looked like a blue smear on the land, something painted on top of the desert. I touched the dry cloth of my one-piece swimming suit. It would be soaking wet on our return trip. Even if it was one-hundred-plus degrees outside, my suit would be cold and give birth to welty hives on my thin body. When I wasn't thinking about this blue-lipped cold or the blue-blue water so out of place, my brother Steve and I listened to our father who was driving and talking about St. Thomas, the pioneer settlement buried under all this blue.

He said the Mormon settlers had been called by church president Brigham Young to build a settlement in this desert and that they had ridden on carts and in wagons drawn by horses and oxen. They crossed the Virgin River and its quicksand at least forty times to get to where they were headed. Then he told us St. Thomas belonged to three different regions in its short life: Utah Territory, Arizona Territory, and finally, Nevada, whose 1864 statehood was rushed to help ensure three electoral votes for Abraham Lincoln's reelection and add to the Republican congressional majorities to garner enough votes to pass the Thirteenth Amendment. A few years later, when the silver boom crashed and the miners left for better places, there would not have been enough citizens to qualify for statehood. Thus, when the newly minted Nevada looked at all possibilities for revenue from its scant population, its legislative eye landed on St. Thomas. In a final blow to the settlers' will to survive, the politicians levied back taxes to be paid in gold and silver coins. Having next to nothing by way of worldly possessions, these pioneers had no choice but to surrender their burst of civilization and turn back to Utah Territory.

My mind drifted off after hearing about silver and gold,

never having seen gold except maybe a gold tooth. My father carried silver dollars in his pockets and complained they made holes. I needed to think about my agreement with my dad, who said he'd let me swim out to the raft by myself. I would swim to the midway point first—the ropes designating the safe swimming area—and then go all the way to the raft glimmering in the distance with its two-rung ladder and diving board. I was ready to solo. I could roll onto my back if the Australian crawl tired me out, and I knew how to float forever. I'd graduated from Red Cross lessons, and I wasn't afraid of water.

My father parked at Boulder Beach. My brother and I unfolded our sweaty bodies into the sizzling summer day. Steve went off for a swimming lesson after Dad warned me three times to be careful. "I'll have my eye on you, just in case," he added. "But you can do it. Right?"

"Right." I retied my Converses and walked gingerly over the cranky rocks—a tap dancer on a hot skillet. Near the shore, I dropped my towel, a rock on top, and reluctantly removed my shoes, trying not to think about the sizzling rocks I still had to cross and the scorching water near the edge. I worried my bare feet wouldn't last. That I'd never reach the place where the lake bottom disappeared and the blackness beneath signaled it was time to drop, reach out with cupped hands, and kick.

But I could suffer through it all because of the secret I knew: the water was ice-cream-cone cold below the hot surface. It could make me shiver, that perfect hiding place from the overpowering sun. I hobbled out far enough where I could free fall into the water, then swam deeper, eyes closed, to visit the netherworld where St. Thomas used to be. I wondered if the silt grazing my cheeks was once crushed by the hooves of somebody's horse, someone who lived in a place called St. Thomas, wherever it was beneath all of this water.

Midway to the raft, I stopped for a breather at the rope and its buoys, then set out on my biggest adventure of the summer.

Australian crawl for twenty-five strokes. Face in. Face out. Breathe to the side. Face in. Face out. Long arms. Cup your hands. Backstroke for twenty-five. Float: stretch your arms overhead, lie still, feel like a banana peel floating on top, water-resistant, waterproof, not subject to the depths or its creatures. Dive beneath the surface to feel the thrilling cold, but not for long. Keep your eye on the raft.

When I climbed out of the lake via the two-rung ladder hooked over the raft's side, I waved my arms overhead, did a hula dance, and shouted with my biggest voice, my hands a megaphone. "I did it." Daddy heard me. He waved back. Steve cheered, though his voice sounded tiny from that far away.

The victory was shallow, however. No one else had come to the raft yet. No sharing of my victory dance. No cheering. I sat down, dangled my feet over the edge, and wondered if my toes would touch anything to do with St. Thomas. If the ghosts of people who died there might brush against my ankle.

Four

I can still hear wind scraping across the Mojave Desert and charging the windows of my bedroom. I can feel sun scorching the air when I cross asphalt streets barefooted, sometimes on my heels and cramped toes to keep the flat of my foot from frying. Heat pouring down from the sun. Heat from the center of the earth. I try to shut out this inferno by burrowing inside the walls of our house, where I sometimes hear my mother wishing she could leave this alien territory and go where things actually grow.

Even though our mother reclaimed squares of our yard with hens-and-chicks and dusty marigolds, the desert always laid in wait, lapping its dry tongue. It framed our existence and bordered our life, this don't-mess-with-me desert. It never asked for names or made distinctions. It taught solitude: how to watch, look, and listen. It taught that things go on forever against odds. That which survives there teaches one to be grateful for small accomplishments.

Five

I feel it in my bones. I could have been here long before St. Thomas was built. When people weren't counting years by number but by seasons or the position of the sun. So many years mashed-together-by-time ago, I would have made baskets. Winnowing baskets. Burden baskets. Bags and water carriers made of hemp. I have inklings of living with children and my mate on top of a mesa, of cultivating crops of corn and wheat on the flood plain below. Baskets on our backs and our hips and in our hands. Steep edges. Handholds and footholds. Ladders up and down. And a recurring sensation of falling from the edge of this mesa and watching the plains below come closer, magnified.

Our village would have known that water was for everyone to use, no one's to keep, too little of it to squander. After all, the annual cycle of snowmelt and overflowing banks had been repeated for ages, long before engineers had dreams about wedging a dam between canyon walls. The Earth gave this water through wet and dry times. The people shared until others arrived with the idea of keeping it for themselves with darts, stone knives, spears.

I have dreams. I'm being pushed. Backwards. By the shoulders. Strong, hard hands and volcanic-glass eyes and a mouth shouting words I do not understand. I can't tell you who or why, but the one who pushes is not someone I know. I only see a blur of colors. Stripes. Xs. Feathers caught in a spin mixed with sunlight. A kaleidoscope. I feel the power of hands pushing against me. Backing me to that edge. The sensation of going back and back when I want to go forward, when I push hard against those hands and yet have no strength to change direction. Everything in this dream pauses while I am airborne, a bird with wide wings, flying past the edge. Arms and legs weightless. Suspended. Full of the lightness of air. When my flight ends, I am falling. Rolling. Crumpling. Splintering.

My family and the others would have to find something better, to weave baskets elsewhere. Basket makers, Pueblo, and Anasazi, coming and going, coming back again and leaving again. Small bands of humans like tides. Like waves. Like water.

Six

Each road sign I pass looks vulnerable all by itself, standing tough against wind and rain and rust, that solitary piece of metal bolted to a post set deep into the ground. It's lonely out here. Maybe I shouldn't be traveling alone on a puny bicycle across the face of this huger-than-huge desert. No cell phone service out here. Something could happen.

The remains of St. Thomas are somewhere in the middle of islands of dusty blue mountains, stony fortresses which rule this land, never letting anyone penetrate, not really, except to tease a few explorers, miners, and spelunkers, people scratching at their surface before retreating. I might have lived here, too, in that first, brief settlement of St. Thomas, or in nearby Callville or St. Joseph—those brief sketches of community on this broad landscape. Before there were paved roads like the one on which I'm now riding. Before there were speed limits or road signs that said, "Callville Bay, 25 miles" or "Las Vegas, 50 miles," though there aren't many of those even now. My mind can see a crumbling adobe doorstep, a cup of water with red silt at the bottom, and a line strung for drying clothes. Small wisps of memory floating up from my subconscious, unconscious, my bones, whatever it is that keeps such secrets.

The pioneers, the salt miners, and the cotton fields are gone. East of here, Las Vegas and its glitter white out the night sky. North of here in Overton, Logandale, and Mesquite, a few farmers and ranchers came back after a while, retrenched the irrigation ditches, planted alfalfa crops, built horse pastures for Arabians, and a few casinos besides. But here in the heart of nothingness, the land is still boss. Just as it was then. Just as it will always be.

I leave the entrance to the Lake Mead National Recreation Area behind, thinking about flash floods, trying not to worry. All around, the land stretches uphill toward the peaks that tower above flat mesas with withered sides. It lifts. It rises, as if a humble servant to the ragged mountaintops jutting above cracked hills of limestone. The land lifts its beds of lava upon which the sun's face mirrors itself at sunset. It lifts the mesquite bushes, the gullies, its stretch marks. Always unflat. Everywhere diagonal. A tilt. This road is a ribbon through moonscape. My feet go round and around, pedaling endlessly. The ligaments, the bones, the muscles straining with every spin cycle. And then I see the sign. "St. Thomas." An arrow pointing east.

Seven

There were two rivers in 1865—the Muddy and the Virgin—both of which flowed eventually into the Colorado River. They are still here—a trickle in some years, a torrent in others—but their confluence and the remains of St. Thomas disappeared when Lake Mead swelled larger than all three rivers, crept up to the doorsteps, into the kitchens and the bedrooms of St. Thomas.

Eight

I dismount. The wooden sign at the back of the asphalt parking lot says: "St. Thomas – 1 Mile." The trail is made of lumpy and dried mud, difficult to negotiate in my bicycle shoes with metal clips on the bottom. A storm is threatening: skies with towering black blossoms of clouds ready to spew their insides onto this land devoid of trees with roots.

I have seen these skies before. I respect them. Their flash floods can sweep away villages, pottery, mortar and pestles made from stone. Even children. They laugh at the people squatting on the land, trying to find a livelihood from so little.

When I was twelve, our family's car, but for a one-second difference, would have been buried beneath a rampage of mud and boulders cascading off an escarpment at the edge of the road. All of this in the mountains on the other side of Las Vegas. Mt. Charleston. To the west instead of to the east where I'm riding today. I stared out the back window to watch a road fill with water and mud-covered rocks pouring off the hillside, plus one singular and significant boulder that bumped the back fender of our car. It rocked us. It stalled our car. Our friends, stopped and stunned on the other side of the sea of debris, had no way to move forward. We waited until dusk for the road-clearing machines to save them.

But it's not a good time to be thinking. Pay attention to the trail. Hurry. I don't get here often. I won't be back soon. I need to see the remains. I can beat the rain.

Nine

In 1871, the settlers of St. Thomas left it all behind—the brutal temperatures, the saline water and alkaline soil, the aggravated Southern Paiute people who tried to steal back what had been taken from them. After six years of hard work, based on a belief that it was God's purpose to make this desert blossom and thus hasten the Second Coming of Christ, they, with the exception of one family, departed. The final blow had been administered by the new state of Nevada, which gerrymandered St. Thomas into its borders. The state maintained the settlers had no legal right to the land, having occupied it by squatters' rights. Surveyors clinched the deal.

A year earlier, when Brigham Young visited the settlers for the first time, he apologized with his hat in hand, a scratch of his beard, the palm of his hand against his face, and a sorry look in his eyes. He said he'd made a mistake in asking them to come to this miserable, inhospitable place without having seen it for himself. He'd relied on misinformed counsel. He was wrong. He couldn't believe all they'd gone through. They'd done more than anyone should have asked. He advised them to leave in peace and trust they had given their best effort. God bless them that day and always.

A few years ago, I discovered that my great-great-grand-father was one of these first settlers. He was a mail carrier for St. Thomas, riding his horse through rain, hail, fog, 120-plus-degree temperatures, flash floods, and ruthless winds. I can hear the hoofbeats now, him riding, riding like "The Highwayman," a poem our father once read to us children. My great-great-grand-father must have ridden on tracks of hardened dirt, delivering letters to a string of people stretched from Callville to Fort Vegas, to the people pitting themselves against this raw land, laughing when they could, dancing their troubles away on Saturday nights if a fiddler could be found. My ancestor would have been dependable. On time, rain or shine. Hardfisted with the reins in his hands for days on end. I can almost smell him: leather, hard trails through sage, caked dust, and his horse. I wonder how he dealt with the news that he and his third wife had lost their only child. Dysentery. Bad water. Not enough water. A man who so wanted to help build the Kingdom of God by contributing his seed to the effort.

Ten

In between tufts of tamarisk, I catch glimpses of the dark blue expanse of Lake Mead—the snowmelt, the springs, the rivers, the floods. I see the reflection of the clouded sky and think of mountains with snow, freezing and melting, tumbling down creases, folds, and crevices into rivers. Gathering momentum. Thundering toward the desert and the Pacific, to the cattle, the growers of fruit trees, the farmers, the cities, the turbines in the dams.

I wish I could have seen the Colorado the way it was before Lake Mead. At my first swimming lessons at Boulder Beach, my father, who wore high-waisted swim trunks over his square hips, the sparse hair on his pale chest rarely exposed to the sun, told me that even though the top of the water was hot, if I dove down into the dark-green depths, I might find the real Colorado River. It was there, somewhere.

The persistent, pesky branches of tamarisk shrubs are taller than I am. I swat them out of my face and curse the government land managers who brought them from Asia to prevent erosion. They're out of control. They've taken over. They're everywhere, on both sides of the stiff-mud dried path once buried beneath the lake.

When I arrive at what is left of St. Thomas, I walk past one foundation—a square made of river stones. Maybe it was the two-story school I read about in the museum. No walls. No windows or anyone looking back at me. Beyond that, an L— half of a square. A smaller square. The water of the lake only three yards away lapping insistently. A bit unnerving. And who would have lived in this house, the one whose cellar is filled with cracked mud? The Perkins? The Briggs? The Kartchners? The Gibbons?—names I read in a list at the museum. When I see the few remains of the effort spent building this town, I feel a sudden regret, though why should I care? I am removed by more than 150 years from these names I'll never know except in historical accounts, my great-great-grandfather a footnote. A few scribbles here and there. A list. A census. A family recording of names. Names with no bodies. Names on paper. Names, names.

Even though the desert makes me think that names don't matter, maybe they do. St. Thomas matters. Lake Mead matters. But only for a little while. Instead of *X* marking the spot, these places have an identity. Their names are a touch point for the rest of us. Their names make them more real, designated as something rather than nothing, a recognition of those who were here, those who gave of their strength, their time, their all, what else could they do?

Before I turn to go back, I listen to the water a few feet from me. Now that I've found it, I no longer feel the need for St. Thomas but rather a strange hope for a record snowfall this year in the mountains whence I came. Precious water. Life-giving water. For all who need the rain, the floods, the snows.

The skies are bursting. I walk, then run, as raindrops splash my hair and clothes and cover my biking gloves with spots of dark gray. Almost out of breath from my sudden burst of "I've got to beat the rain," I reach my bike. I look back one more time at the always surprising expanse of the lake, so much blue at the bottom of land slanting every which way toward the original riverbed. The Spanish and the geologists call these slopes *bajada*, the slanting formations that make this place crooked and off-kilter. Gratefully, the rain is warm and steady. Not harsh. Twenty miles to go. I won't drown or be swept away.

Eleven

The remains of St. Thomas have brought me to breathe the clear desert air once again and to be wary of holes where scaly creatures watch for intruders. This is my land—this sand, these rocks, these weeds that dry up and tumble—even though it is called a land best left to itself.

I could have been a Native woman with red paint smeared across my cheeks who understands the barren, never-ending hills and that there are others/other natives/other tribes that want what I have coaxed from the land when need is stark.

I could have been a pioneer woman, building an adobe house, birthing and burying.

I was a child splashing in the waters of Lake Mead with my father standing close by.

I am a woman wondering about the naming of names and the busyness of human effort to subdue the earth and engineer it into something habitable.

Call me whatever you want. I don't need a name. Names are useful for a while—the ones found on dried scraps of paper, on pages in books in libraries and museums and on microfiche—in between floods and sandstorms. The wind will blow. It will tear paper that the sun has yellowed and curled at the edges. The rain will fall. Water will blur the ink. Whatever names we call ourselves and those who came before us, they remind us what has been here, what preceded us. Names. Yes, names. Transient, flying-through-the-sky-blowing-in-the-dust names.

My real father/mother/lover is the wind, the sun, the smell of water gathering in clouds, the curtains of rain. I am a creature made of lizard skins, sagebrush, horsetail grass, and rain-washed sand. Once in a while I flash brilliance, like heat lightning or the pink prickly pear blossom, but mostly I'm subtle like the desert and this dust. My land which can never be owned.

I have been here before. I am here now. I will leave again. Following the way of the desert.

GREAT BASIN DNA

Chloe and Henry, my grandparents, lie buried in the Idaho earth (as do most of their ten children). Thora, their daughter and my mother, however, escaped Idaho. During her first and only year of college, she found a nothing-to-do-with-farming husband—a wandering Mormon who was kind, charming, and sensitive; a daydreaming man of the mind. They married. They moved to Ely, Nevada, to the ancient seabed of the Great Basin.

Thora left irrigation ditches, burly brothers who teased her mercilessly, cows' udders, an early-to-bed and early-to-rise schedule for a bigger life, but gradually grew disenchanted with that vast 225,000-mile stretch between the Rockies and the Sierra Nevadas, the Mojave Desert and the Columbia Plateau, that large sink where things struggled to survive and where everything turned to dust and was picked up by the hot wind she secretly hoped would blow her back to Idaho when the time was right.

Despite her good intentions, Mother's allegiance was to Idaho. Even though she lived in different places in Nevada for much longer than she ever lived in Idaho, something in her never moved there. Her heart and mind were attached to the backside view of the Grand Tetons with its tumbling streams and profoundly mysterious peaks—the place where she was born. Something about her felt she had been abandoned by her high hopes to a land better meant for snakes and lizards, to a man who didn't understand how to bring prosperity into their lives. She was a woman split in the middle. A woman longing for a semblance of home and stability, despite its drawbacks. A woman wanting a chance to be something more. A woman passing this split on to her children.

○

Every summer, the sun's magna rays blasted our mint-green automobile as it crossed the southern tip of Nevada and headed north on Highway 91. Mother poured water from our thermos onto clean diapers, and we three kids in the back seat hung them over the window glass to cool things off. That helped, primitive air conditioning that it was. We were making our annual trek: Idaho, Idaho, always Idaho. Mom wouldn't go anywhere else, though we couldn't afford to take another kind of vacation.

Our father belonged to the desert. He didn't fit in with the Idaho farmers, their tractors, or their good-old-boy, clap-their-hand-on-the-back affability. He taught us the beauty of the barren. While he steered our car past Mesquite, through St. George, and past the west side of Zion National Park on our northbound trek, he made attempts to open the eyes and minds of his three children who sat in the back seat of the boiling car, the baby in the front seat on Mother's lap. "Did you know that this is all part of the Great Basin that makes up most of Nevada, Utah, parts of Oregon, California, and a little bit of Idaho?" he'd say. "Did you know that the desert has many interesting secrets it keeps to itself?"

But we all secretly knew that southeastern Idaho was where the earth was solid and real, the people made of earth, not vapor. He wasn't fooling us.

"I haven't talked to my mother in such a long time," Mother said, balancing baby Kathy on her lap and passing out her roast beef sandwiches, the meat sliced from a roast she'd cooked the night before, the lettuce, sliced tomatoes, and pickles stacked high on bread she'd made and slathered with mustard and mayonnaise. "I wish long-distance calls weren't so expensive. I wish we didn't live so far away."

"But we do," our dad would say. "We live in a place with opportunity. We're not enclosed in a box."

"Funny," she said, her voice sounding wistful like the wind gentling around a corner. "I always said that I'd never marry a farmer. But I miss the animals, the streams and meadows, the new-mown hay. I can't wait to see Lloyd and Zenna. Lois. My other brothers. Mother and Dad." Moist tenderness filled her voice as we headed for the solid part of our family—the hardworking farm folks who knew their right foot from their left, who had common sense, and who were masters at putting in a good day's work. Work, work, work. We were headed toward the uncles who wondered if Thora's skinny kids would ever be solid enough to count for much. When these uncles hugged me, they crunched my thin bones together with their broad chests and Superman, hay-baling strength.

Too hot in the car, the three of us fell asleep to the sound of the tires on the pavement, rolling, rolling, rolling. When I woke from my nap, my hair wet from perspiration and mashed flat on one side, we were still driving along the rim of the Great Basin, Dad pointing out the spotty pools at the edge of the Great Salt Lake. "That's what's left of Lake Bonneville," he said. "A sink with no drains or outlets. Said to be here twenty-five thousand years ago. History, kids. You've gotta love history." Steve and I sucked in our cheeks and made fish lips at each other.

But then, quiet as a finger on silk, we slipped over the border into the holy land of Idaho where Thora and her nine siblings were born.

The beginnings of southeast Idaho looked like Mars magnified. Moon surface. Cratered, acne-like pits on its face. Lumpy. Massive stretches of lava looking black and searing in the summer sun. Tiptoe barefoot across that territory and die. What happened here? Tyrannosaurus rex, pteranodon, what exactly? Everything was craggy and cranky. Bad-tempered landscape, no beaches or groves of trees, just burnt toast, especially in the summertime. But then the land stretched out flat, turning into farmland watered by the Snake River. Our mother's home.

○

There's a struggle in me.

On one hand, Mother was Idaho—earth to be depended on. The butcher, the baker, the candlestick maker, all in one. Fruit pies. Cobblers. Candies. Meringues three inches high. She baked, baked, and baked. Whole wheat bread from wheat she ground. Endless pies. She canned, preserved, jammed, and jellied all summer long. We ate huge breakfasts every day, fit for preparing us to mend fences, keep cattle inside the farm's boundaries, chase chickens, collect eggs, pitch hay, and dig weeds from the garden.

And Mother was Mormon through and through. She once told us that her friend in junior high, maybe because they'd heard about World War I at school, thought the world was made up of Germans and Mormons. Mother laughed about that one, yet in the next breath and in so many words said: "Of course, the way Mormons are supposed to live is the only way to live life." No argument. No debate from us kids. "The church will make you happy." Idaho equals noble relatives, equals stability, equals common sense, equals Mormonism.

She had strong arms, of which she was ashamed, thinking she wasn't as graceful or appealing as she could be without them. She had strong legs that could walk for miles. A healthy heart and lungs. She was dedicated to making things better for her children. It was easy to trust her, even with her strong opinions. She would catch any of us should we fall (though told us we just better not fall). "You get hurt, pick yourself up. Somebody says something mean, forget it. Dust yourself off; turn the other cheek. Don't waste time feeling sorry for yourself."

Then there was my father, an insurance salesman, an ethereal sky of a man whose pastoral life was in his head, not in the fields; a man born to parents who, during his childhood, crisscrossed the Great Basin continuously looking for work in Utah, Nevada, and southeast Idaho. He'd been a boy hanging on to the Mormon religion by a spidery thread; a boy whose father picked up and moved his family endlessly, always looking for a better opportunity. He sold newspapers in the red-light district in Ely, Nevada, and received Christmas candy from the ladies of the night; a scrappy boy whose sisters sang songs in front of taverns for a few much-needed coins. Ultimately, Dad decided that his survival depended on striking out on his own. He wanted to finish college and teach. He wanted to write—to sit in front of his typewriter punching keys instead of cows. He had different visions.

I believed in my father and his dreams that awakened something in me and left my solid mother in the dust. And yet, something in my training, perhaps my mother's wistful stories, led me to conclude that people were more solid who'd been nourished by Idaho—that they were more dependable and principled, that they resembled trees with their deep, dug-down roots. My father and I, seduced by the life of the mind, the place that offered the safest haven for both of us, the quiet contemplation inside our heads, were possibly missing the mark.

As much as I've tended to books and classical music, I know that, buried inside me—the creative thinker, the semi–concert pianist, and a woman with two college degrees—there is a plain-sense woman with wide hips and calluses on her hands that she hides in the pockets of her skirt, a woman dressed in a gingham apron grinding wheat into flour for bread with half-tied work boots on her feet. She is strong like her mother. Her arms can carry heavy things. She isn't afraid of the dark and can kick a fence post with the toe of her boot, even carry a shotgun by her side if she has to. Clear-eyed, no nonsense, no vacillation, she stands for might and right. Untainted. Noble. She cannot tell a lie.

○

We arrived in Idaho Falls, fully reminded of our mother's yearning for the life she once knew, the good life where work was hard but living more simple. Before we reached the turn-off to Iona, we stopped at the swinging bridge stretched over the roaring waterfalls, the bridge that bounced when you walked across and made you think you'd never get home alive, especially when your brother did jumping jacks behind you and both your feet rose up off the bridge and your stomach flip-flopped. Idaho Falls, where the broad Snake ran—a stealthy, swift undercurrent moving along like a plow.

In 1930, when she was a senior in high school, Mother lived near this river. She boarded in the city so she wouldn't have to negotiate the snow and distance from the family farm in Iona every day. After high school she stayed in town, working at the Woods Funeral Home for six dollars a week, deciding not to be afraid of the dead because they weren't as dangerous as the living. The Depression was nothing new to her. She was used to going without and pinching pennies.

She married Herman in 1937 and lived in Nevada until the winter cold of 1943, when Elaine was five and I was seven months old. The three of us moved to Idaho Falls while Dad left to sail the Pacific aboard a tanker ship destined to dodge Japanese Zeroes. Mother had hoped her relatives could help care for me, the baby, when she found a job, but quickly learned the rule about making one's bed and having to lie in it. Her mother had a stroke; her sisters were too busy. After months of scrambling, her brother, Lloyd, recommended her to the school board to teach at Sage Creek, even though she'd had only one year of college. He also offered us a vacant house on his property, one with a well, one bedroom, and an outhouse.

While Mother taught twenty students at the one-room school, her brothers' children and my sister Elaine making up one-fifth of the class, I got ferried around—a pierless boat, bobbing in the water of aunts, friends, babysitters, and a scratch-and-bite nursery school. But in the summertime, Elaine and I played on the earth where potatoes grew, next to the pasture where cows and horses were corralled, where the sharp, pinch-your-nose smell of cow dung stung our eyes. With kitchen spoons, we dug toward the Pacific. We dug for hours, hoping to find Daddy.

At night I could feel a ghost horse's breath on my cheek and hear its exhalations as I dreamed that Daddy held me close to its wet nose. I felt his arms around me and the bottom rail of a pasture fence beneath my feet, where I silently commanded the cattle to come to me—the leader of the herd, a true-blue-straight-through cowgirl. I looked into their wide brown eyes and knew there was a connection between me, the cows, the steers, the calves. We were comrades beneath the vast spread of stars against a clear night sky, no city lights interfering.

Water, the background music to my dream, gurgled outside in the irrigation ditch, the one Mother warned us away from at every opportunity. The sounds of shifting cattle huddling close to the fence, the soft settling of hen's feathers in the chicken house. These things settling my worry about the father who hadn't been kissing my cheek good night for too long.

○

After Idaho Falls, we had three stops to make in Iona. (1) Our grandparents' house for tweaks on our ears and comments about how fast we were growing; (2) Aunt Zenna's and Uncle Bill's, where we ate fresh, cooked vegetables from Zenna's garden, thus learning the attributes of the heretofore scary-red beet before playing with our cousins on dusty, unpaved roads until dusk; (3) Aunt Lois's and Uncle Harold's, where we spent the night because there weren't so many cousins who needed beds at their house.

Both Zenna and Lois lived in basement houses with their husbands and children: root cellar houses with a lonely door sticking out of the ground. When we carried our suitcases inside, we climbed down narrow cement stairs and descended into the wild, cold Idaho earth, feeling like potatoes in a root cellar, always trying to get warm, afraid to put our arms outside the covers when we got in bed. Nonstop shivering. Dead-set chill. That year, however, thanks to good crops, thus more money for people to buy the RVs her husband sold, Lois greeted us in her now-expanded house, now built above ground, now with a warm living room, kitchen, and living quarters for the year-round residents, though still not for us.

After we spent a few days in Iona casing out the two-story, sandstone-block post office/grocery store combo where Steve liked to buy waxy pop-bottle-shaped containers of colored sugar water, after tiptoeing across the curling yellow linoleum in Grandma's kitchen while her canary trilled its song for us, after looking into Grandpa's stereopticon at pictures of Yellowstone and Old Faithful, and after freezing to slow motion in Aunt Lois's basement at night, we were ready for our annual ride in the old yellow school bus Uncle Bill had outfitted.

With as many cousins as could fit, we partied all the way to the ranch—playing pinochle, War and Fish, War and Clue, more War, telling jokes, the kids sometimes sleeping on the few bus seats left on the bus, while our transport passed rows of lodge-pole pines. But this year, we were told at the last minute that the bus had broken down. Everyone had to take their own car for the annual pilgrimage to Uncle Lloyd's summer ranch just west of West Yellowstone: the stellar, star-on-top-of-the-tree, big event of our annual summer vacation.

On Highway 20, we drove northeast through miles of evergreens, the shadow and the sun striping the road. We paused at Henry's Fork to watch the fishermen on the bridge, angling after those silvery, slippery fish, then drove on to Mack's Inn: the symbol of almost-being-there. We were anxious to come to the open stretch where the fields stretched toward the hills, where barbed wire fences hung from one end of the open plain to the other, and where we'd turn off the highway and drive down the dirt road to the red-roofed house and the green-roofed lodge, our car raising dust that erased the numbers on our Nevada license plates.

Solid, tall, lit-by-sunshine, big-hearted Uncle Lloyd had been out checking on his cattle, but when he saw that we'd arrived, he galloped toward us on his black, silky horse, Midnight. Our motor was still ticking when we piled out of the smelly car with its remnants of spilled milk, diapers, and furtive farts. He wore a plaid shirt with snap-on buttons and a pair of hard-as-iron fabric slacks. He wore chaps over his slacks. He was a real cowboy, and we were all in awe. He was the brother most attentive to my mother. He was the brother my mother was most attentive to. In fact, Mother worshiped him. When I saw him in the saddle, I thought of a king on a steed, like I'd read about in books. I was stirred by the sight of our royal lineage. The year before I'd seen Mother riding beside Uncle Lloyd, amazed at how queenly she looked in the saddle—Mother's home once upon a time. That meant there were ranchers and cowgirls in our blood. Maybe some kings and queens, too.

Uncle Lloyd hugged Mother, lifted her off the ground, and whirled her around. He shook hands with Dad, squeezed his shoulder with his strong hand, and I saw my father wince just a little. Then Lloyd hugged us green-behind-the-ears desert rats who'd come a long way to play cowboys and rustlers.

"So, how are you kids doing?" he asked, patting us on the back and smiling that cowboy-used-to-sun-and-rain-and-all-kinds-of-weather smile.

"Great," we said, then scattered—the aunts to the ranch house kitchen to unpack the groceries and make plans for the evening meal, Uncle Lloyd to catch some fish for dinner in the stream running through the meadow, the children to the lodge with our suitcases.

○

Mother seemed less anxious when she could be with her brother in her true home of Idaho. Lloyd had succeeded in the world. A stalwart in both church and community. Strong. Sure. Plainspoken. He knew how to manage land, crops, and herds. He loved God and wasn't afraid to say so and liked country music on his truck radio. An amiable, natural-boss kind of cowboy, good to the bone, he sometimes giggled in a boyish voice when he kidded around with us nieces and nephews. Pure solid.

All of us kids felt at home on Lloyd's ranch. We hiked through the trees on a deer trail. We ate meat, potatoes, and fresh vegetables in the red-roofed kitchen. We slept in the green-roofed lodge. Its bannisters were made of twisted tree branches with the nubs still intact where smaller branches had been sawed off, their bark barely removed and patchy in places. Dead trees provided our lodging, gave their lives for us and for the returning queen, our mother. Her strength was here. She never should have left after World War II with our dad, determined to live his own life. She should have stayed in the pure, solid state of Idaho. The Great Basin was for the dead bones of fish, crabs, and spiny lobsters—the world of the once-upon-a-time sea, now dry and cracked.

○

The lodge was a big hull of a place with planked flooring hewn by a slightly unsteady hand. It smelled stale after being closed up all winter. Its stairs creaked and groaned that too many people with too many bags had come to stay. There was the scurry of soft-footed mice. The sounds of suitcases being unlatched next to the beds with assorted pastel-colored chenille bedspreads and sagging, squeaky springs.

Outside, the newly arrived cousins ran until our legs almost fell off, and after dinner, we anticipated an evening of charades and the cousins' annual invitation to a snipe hunt. We'd fallen for that trick once and followed them out in the trees to look for that rare find of a bird. They got a good laugh on us city kids. But tonight, we asked Uncle Lloyd to tell us the story of Uncle Russell. "Please, tell us again, oh please," we joined in a cousins' chorus.

"Well," Uncle Lloyd began, the fireplace crackling with burning logs and a passel of cousins sitting cross-legged on the braided rugs, "A big storm had moved in. Pelting rain ready to launch. Russell worried about one of the sheep that hadn't come back with the herd. Nobody could tell him any different, strong-headed like he was, so he set out to rescue that lamb. Wanted to bring it home before the storm hit too hard."

I pictured the deluge, the big drops beating down the brim of Russell's felt hat and dripping onto his long slicker.

"Storm clouds were coming in fast. Russell must have been cresting the hill near a lone tree because that's where we found him. He was struck clean-through by lightning, his boots blown out at the soles." He paused. The room was quiet except for the fire, and in the stillness, I knew he still missed Russell.

"You know I keep that saddle," he said, a flatness in his usually twinkling eyes.

"Can we see it again?" Steve and I said carefully, not to seem too anxious about seeing our favorite artifact.

"Maybe not tomorrow, but before you go," Lloyd said. "Time to say good night and turn in. Work starts early around here."

Everyone shuffled off to brush their teeth in a wash basin and hurry to the frigid outhouse to pee, then snuggled into one of the double beds scattered through the upstairs of the lodge. More heavy quilts up to our chins; the weight made our feet spread out like duck feet. Settling into sleep, I thought about the saddle. I'd seen it before—a star drilled through the leather right where Russell would have been riding, an uneven star with more than the five points of the lick-em, stick-em stars our teachers gave out at school. I couldn't wait to see it again. Who else in this world got to see the evidence of lightning, its footprint, its tracks after the big rumble in the sky and the crooked spear of blinding white light struck?

The next morning, Uncle Lloyd went off to move some cattle to another grazing spot and instructed his two sons, Lynn and Dale, to saddle up some ponies for the city slickers to have a ride around the pasture. These ponies knew how to pretend, for a few minutes at least, that we were their boss. We trotted, bounced, and slammed into the saddle. I hugged my pony's sides with my knees—my thighs trembling from the effort before long—and used the reins with little success. My pony knew a novice wrangler on her back and chose the direction she pleased.

After the ponies were de-saddled and released to their pasture, a group of cousins suggested we go into the hills and look for tracks—bear, deer, and elk. But Dale, his horse's reins still in his hand, pulled me aside. "Do you want to go for a ride?" he asked. "We can catch up with them later." He was my same age—both of us eleven, soon to hit twelve.

"For sure," I said.

"Do you think it's a good idea to wear those shorts?" he asked. "Not much protection."

"Why not?" I said defiantly, defending my skimpy Las Vegas attire. I was a City Girl. He needed to remember that.

He shrugged his shoulders, mounted his horse, then helped me stand in the stirrup where I could swing my right leg to the other side. We headed for the ridge of trees thick in the distance. We jumped streams, picked our way around coils of barbed wire, negotiated the ups and downs, and were soon slithering through the thickness of trees.

Suddenly, a broken-off branch sticking out straight from a tall pine dug into the top of my thigh. Hard. Dragged its broken tip across my leg, drew drops of bright-red blood across my olive and sun-tanned skin, and made a wet necklace, evenly spaced. I refused to cry or to let Dale know he had a wounded passenger. Fighting an almost uncontrollable urge to bleat my pain, I didn't moan, complain, or grind my teeth. I sat tall in my Nevada short shorts, trying not to wince. I avoided looking at the long, deep scratch, where my blood seeped and beaded.

○

Because we were taking our annual family tour to Yellowstone the next day, there was no chance to see Uncle Russell's saddle. Elaine, Steve, and I were bickering more than usual when we climbed into the suffocating back seat, and I was in a wicked mood, telling everyone to stay clear of my bandaged leg. But we managed to listen to our dad's instructions as we entered the park. "Keep your windows rolled up. The bears look friendly, but they're not teddy bears. If they come up to the car, just stay inside." Lucky for us, some bears did saunter past our car, about five feet from us, and we got a close look at their snouts and their button-black eyes. We also spotted lots of buffalo near the Old Faithful Lodge, herds of elk, and deer everywhere. The day turned out after all, but as we drove back to the ranch, I was thinking about the saddle. We'd be leaving for Nevada in the morning.

I got out of bed early on the last day to watch the sun blossom into the wide-open sky. I loved the pale oranges and whispery blues of morning, the sound of the creek, the sight of grass bending in the morning breeze, graceful as a geisha dancer I'd seen on the fan Daddy brought back from China. Without waking anyone, I pulled on my T-shirt, blue jeans, and Keds, crept down the stairs, and slipped out the front door. I looked up and down the long road and decided to walk all the way back to the highway, which was at least a mile if not more. A few deer leapt across the pasture, heading for the trees. Two elk grazed. A flock of birds swooped to the only telephone wire leading to Lloyd's house. My soul started to sing. I could hear it.

When I saw a huddle of cows close to the fence that ran along the side of the road, I decided to check out something I'd suspected. With calmer-than-calm silence, I climbed up on the bottom rail of the fence and stood there without moving one muscle. In my mind, I commanded the brown, shaggy cattle to come to me. And they did. Slowly, curiously, not even hesitantly. It was like they knew me and were coming over to say, "Don't leave us, cowgirl."

I wasn't sure where this magic power came from, but it was almost as if I had a secret cow whistle built into my thoughts or some giant magnet welded to my backbone. They kept coming like a bunch of bony boys shuffling their feet, keeping their options open. I looked into their eyes when they came close. I had no sugar cubes, but they stood there, chewing grass and mooing once in a while, until I raised both of my arms, held them high in freeze motion, then shook my hands once to release them. The spell was broken. I hopped down from the fence. Maybe I really was an Idaho girl. Maybe I did belong here.

When I arrived at the lodge, everyone had loaded their suitcase into the car except for me. "Where were you?" Mother asked, an edge to her voice, "and why are you always taking off without telling me where you're going?" But then Kathy was crying, and when Mother turned her attention to calming the baby, I slid off the hook.

"Hey, kids." Uncle Lloyd came out of his house toward our car. "Do you have a minute to see the saddle I promised to show you?" Of course, we all nodded. He walked toward a small, square shed, pulled a huge chunk of keys out of his pocket, and unlocked the padlock on the door. The sunlight streamed inside the chilly room that had no overhead lights. In half-shadow and half-light, sunbeams filtering through the cracks between the planks of the wall, we saw the sacred saddle. It sat on a sawhorse. It needed to be dusted. "There it is," Uncle Lloyd said, and none of us said much of anything. We were in the presence of something holier than holy. I hesitated, then asked if I could touch the hole, the star, the tracks left by the lightning. I'd wanted to do that for a long time. "Fine with me," he said.

Time slowed. My finger moved across space that seemed like forever until I touched the saddle. I was touching the finger of God that tapped Uncle Russell on the shoulder. I was connected to the stem of lightning stretching from heaven to the earth to jolt Uncle Russell into heaven, connected to his presence up in the sky, his hope that we'd all live good enough lives to see him again. I lifted my finger. It left a dark smudge on the leather. I licked my fingertip to taste lightning. I tasted dust.

After we climbed back into the car and said goodbye to the cousins, aunts, and uncles, the horses, the cattle, the fences, the trees, I slid to the corner away from Elaine and Steve to think thoughts on dust. Every time when we drove the dirt road that turned back onto Highway 20, the road that left the ranch behind, I felt strongly that this was how land was supposed to be, not some godforsaken bottom of some abandoned sea with trilobites encased in dry mud. Not in between shifting hills of sand, not at the mercy of flash floods and violent temperatures. We were safe at Uncle Lloyd's ranch and definitely safer than we were in Nevada. The rivers were regular in Idaho. Rocks and rills, like in the song. The pine trees tall and protective. We didn't have to cool our rooms with a swamp cooler. We didn't have to stay inside during the summer days to keep from burning up.

I wanted to claim this territory as mine, to lay claim to the thousands-of-acres fact that we were related to something this vast. My father could never make the kind of living that would support a ranch such as this. He must have had to talk to himself hard about things not being roses anywhere. What was so great about Idaho? Why did Thora, one of her sisters, and two of her six brothers leave?

As we drove back to the shores of Lake Bonneville, back to the land of lizards and snakes, where the few plants that could survive on an old ocean floor had to convince themselves it was safe to grow there, I knew that, as much as I'd like to pretend otherwise, I'd forever be a child of that scrappy geography. A child covered with lizard scales, with a little cowhide mixed in.

In the car, motoring toward the sweltering heat of summer, my fingertips brushed over the bumpy remains of the necklace scar on my leg. I counted twelve pearl-like scabs. Dad was telling us that he'd take us to the dry lake just outside of Boulder City to search for trilobites left behind during the vast evaporation when wind and sun carried the water elsewhere.

THE DESERT, WAITING

can feel the sun boiling my skin, even now when I think about it. Turning it red. Scalding me from above. Sometimes there was more than the heat over my head and all around my body—something malignant boiling beneath the Mojave Desert, something below the sand and the rocks. Unbearable heat rose from the magma underneath the surface, and then there were the pictures I'd seen—waterfalls of lava splashing and leaping uncontrollably on the inside of the earth.

Was that the hell I'd heard talked about? People were good at throwing around that word, that idea, that place. H-E-double-toothpicks, the proper people would call it, and some felt constrained never to say the word at all. I'd heard about it, wherever, whatever it was, and this heat certainly felt like the fires of hell at times—Satan, Lucifer, Beelzebub, and the Prince of Darkness reigning in that very hot place. You'd wish you'd never been sent there. Burning in hell. Flames licking at your elbows while the Devil laughs to have you, at last, in his hooks.

That hell, after World War II, 1950, when I was about seven years old, wasn't always a subject in the four walls of that small LDS ward building in Boulder City, Nevada. It wasn't only a religious topic. Trust me. Even the kids at school had something to say about hell. But the talks at church in sacrament meeting (given by whomever from the congregation the bishop asked to speak on a particular Sunday) seemed to be more about the three glories—the telestial (the lowest of the three kingdoms, for liars, sorcerers, adulterers, whoremongers, and whosoever loves and makes a lie), the terrestrial (the middle degree for those who were blinded by the craftiness of men and thus rejected the fullness of the gospel of Jesus Christ), and, of course, the celestial—the one that's the Mormons' highest heaven. I never heard that much about "hell" when I went to church.

But once in the Boulder City Ward, this old-timer who lived in McKeeversville—the shanty town built around the railroad tracks when Hoover Dam was being built and which is no longer in existence—stood at the pulpit, raised his finger, and talked about Sons of Perdition, eternal fire, and damnation. His words scared me, that's the truth. And the world didn't feel as safe after that. He was big, a giant of a man, I remember. He wore overalls sometimes and liked to clean the wax out of his ears with one finger. He took us children for rides around the park across from our church. We squeezed into the rumble seat in the back of his 1931 Ford coupe where its inverted trunk caused us no end of joy as we rode in the open air, wind blowing our hair every which way, giggling to feel so free and heedless and privileged. But when he was speaking to the congregation on that day, the ceiling fan turning fruitlessly over our heads and our mothers cooling themselves with fold-up paper fans they kept in their purses, he pointed the same finger that cleaned his ear at all of us sitting below the stage where the pulpit was situated. Little pitchers with big ears, you know. I was too young to distinguish between attitude, opinion, truth, and reality, and even now, I'm unsure. Is hell a for-real place? Did that old-timer know what he was talking about?

This is the harder part, though—to tell you that this desert also reminded me of God, who, I was taught, is all-powerful in the heavens and much bigger than all of us. Who, if not He, decided there should be such a thing as the desert? God created all of this. He's the head of everything. And God must have had something to do with the Three Nephites—the three mortals ordained to live forever by Jesus when he appeared in the Book of Mormon (3 Nephi: 28). They "never taste of death . . . until all things will be fulfilled according to the will of the Father."

So why was the heat so hard on me? Why did I think it would be bad news to be stranded all by myself outside in this barren place, this Mojave Desert, when there were Three Nephites who watched after you? I should have been faithful and trusting and believing that one of them would show up if I was in trouble, just like the stories I'd heard in Primary and testimony meeting where anyone who wanted to stood at the pulpit and bore witness to the truthfulness of the Gospel. There were some good stories at those once-a-month testimony meetings, and who could predict what some people would say? They'd talk about their trips to Provo and Salt Lake, the way their car broke down and was then magically fixed after they prayed over the hood. They'd talk about how their son had been violently ill and had then been blessed by someone in the priesthood and how he'd revived. Sometimes, even men would cry when they talked about their families and what they believed was the truth. I liked that men felt comfortable with tears in their eyes because I always got choked up myself when I spoke—part and parcel of the process. When I got older, though, I started to feel this moisture in my eyes and my voice was more habitual than something real.

But back to the Three Nephites. I remember one of those stories. A man was wandering in the desert—dazed and confused, thirsty unto total dryness, ready to give up, probably crawling on his hands and knees in torn clothes, his tongue almost hanging out for want of a sip of water. And, voila, he was found by one of those Nephites, who led him back to civilization. There were tons of those miraculous stories flying around when I was young, such as the one about a man who was prompted to get out of bed and move his wagon one night. He followed the prompting, and, the next morning, found a tree toppled over onto the spot where the wagon had been sitting. These stories used to send shivers down my spine, so I must have believed them. But I guess I must not have been full of complete faith at the time because I thought maybe I could melt before anyone would arrive to save me.

I've been caught in the crosshairs of this zenith and nadir, this zone between heaven and hell, this questioning, this probing of what the truth is. This heat and this desert is part of me. It pounded on my shiny black hair and felt like fire when I didn't wear shoes and skittered barefoot across asphalt. I first negotiated those streets named Arizona, Utah, California, New Mexico, etc. (after the seven states where the Colorado River flows) as a young girl in Boulder City, the town built to build Hoover Dam. Later, in Las Vegas, where we moved when I was eleven (before Howard Hughes, the hotel boom on the Strip, and the Mafia—I'd only heard about this organization through the grapevine so don't know that one for sure), I negotiated narrower but still hot streets. Dressed in a T-shirt, short shorts, and bare feet—sometimes on my heels and cramped toes curled to keep my soles from frying—I could feel heat everywhere: on my head, my arms, my hands, my torso, my everything. Bully of all bullies. That heat. It could hard-boil an egg in the shell. It could hard-boil me. Hot, hot, hot, as if there were no other word in the dictionary. Hot, hot, hot, like the hell some people talked about.

On the worst days, I'd retreat to my house—my safe place. I burrowed inside four walls behind a closed door and lay on top of my bed with a book and pinned curls hopeful against limpness. While my mother rattled pans in the kitchen and I settled my neck on the pillow that became increasingly wet, I'd bet she was wishing, as she often did, that she could move back North where things survived, where life seemed more plentiful and generous. Idaho was her heaven, the place where her family worked their fingers to the bone harvesting potatoes, running farms and ranches, and selling RVs. They were a step above the angels with their stiff upper lips, their goodness, and their dedication to the word of the Lord. Somehow, they seemed set apart from southern Nevada and the rest of the lone and dreary world that sometimes felt like hell. I think we secretly worshiped the relatives in Idaho and thought they were more stable than we would ever be. We could blow away while they were digging potatoes.

I'd watched my mother plenty of times, coaxing her plants and trying to encourage things in hardscrabble plots—hens-and-chicks and dusty marigolds, sometimes even sweet peas. She stood for hours with a garden hose filling dry rings dug around the base of her two fruit trees, determined to have peaches and apricots she could preserve in jars for her family that wouldn't stop growing. But the desert didn't have much to give in the way of moisture. Only water from the hose saved those trees. Water brought in from somewhere else.

I should tell you it wasn't always as hot as I'm saying, though there were plenty of hot days. There were alluring days, in fact, and indelible memories in those summer times, like standing in front of swamp coolers on high with my cheeks feeling the breeze, and like me and my siblings turning a baked-adobe brown when we ran outside. And, I was certain. I had answers. To everything, even though I was a skinny, scrawny, loosely-pieced-together kid. I thought I knew so much. Maybe because my religion had all of the answers to everything. THE TRUTH. Or because of my father, the proud and humble bishop who stood in front of the congregation every week, the man respected, the man listened to, and the man who cared for his flock of sheep and was as kind as anyone I ever knew. Was I blessed among the children of humans to know where we came from and where we were going, or was I a product of the simple arrogance that came with being in what I considered the top echelon of my ward, of even more than my ward? I think, perhaps, I had a smidge, if not more, of pride, a streak of self-importance. After all, it is a big statement to say that you KNOW, that you KNOW, WITHOUT A DOUBT, the truth, even if it is outlined by the Church of Jesus Christ of Latter-day Saints and verified by the twelve current apostles and the head of the church known as the Prophet.

But the desert tempered all of that, sometimes in a succulent, generous, breathtaking way; sometimes in a frightening, windblown way. The desert was unpredictable. No mind could fathom its wiles, just as, I happen to think, no mind can fathom who and what God was or is. Our minds are fallible. They are finite. Infinity is an entirely different thing. We can only guess at what lies in store. The desert told me that.

On warm nights, my brother, sister, and I slept outside in a double bed and listened to sprinklers and smelled water at work while we basked in the night sky with its scattering of stars. We listened to crickets and pretended we owned it all until other insects discovered the innards of the mattress. But when we moved to Las Vegas, the wind blew almost incessantly and the streetlights and the neon from the Strip changed the number of stars we could see—another unwanted reminder of the Devil and the unfairness of living in such a skimpy habitat where the wind whined and shrieked around corners of our tract home.

We lived on the edge of town facing an empty desert. Our two-story house was covered with yellow stucco and bordered by hard-packed dirt, a clothesline, the hopeful sticks of an apricot and a peach tree, a fence of stacked bricks, and a sad garden. The wind pummeled the bedroom windows with sand. "I'm boss here!" it seemed to shout as it bent shrubs flat—the ones across the street, the creosote, mesquite, the tumbleweeds before they tumbled. It puffed the clouds away, too, swept the valley clean, uncovered the sun, and made the hills and mountains as sharp as the edge of a serrated knife. It was stronger than my thin, skinny body, which would blow away if I stood out in the open without a wall at my back. It was bigger than I was, that's for sure, and it could push me to places I never asked to go. It could be God or Satan, this unmanaged power, this fierceness.

During a winter day, the sky could be steel slate with almost no delineation of clouds, wind blowing against the gray cover but not able to make a dent. I could hear the chorus of clouds being crowded into that big one, those commentators, as they expressed themselves from the underbelly of the sky, mumbling what the answer to all of it was though I could never quite understand what they said. What did it all mean? It seemed so pushy. But maybe this was a show to scare tiny mortals who dot the landscape with their cars, houses, and dreams of what it was all about. How important were we, are we? The desert goes on and on, miles and miles, impersonal. We try, but fail, to own it, to wrestle it to its knees.

Not much water ever made it to the ground. Not much rain. "Oh, please rain today," I'd pray. "If not rain, at least a few clouds please," though even clouds were less than a real threat. Once in a surprising while there was too much rain. Flash floods. Feast or famine. I remember a raging river in front of our house, too swift for swimming, but an awesome sight for my eyes that were hankering for water. I expected to see floating animals being carried by the current. Floating refrigerators. Floating boats, but all I remember was the water, the rush of it, the brown of it. Bigger and starker than I could imagine. A river on East St. Louis Street in Las Vegas, Nevada.

But the sunsets offset this *sturm und drang*. Nothing was or is more beautiful. Nothing. The sky could be vivid, alight, vibrant, on fire, a mass of yellow, orange, reds, purples, you name it, even chartreuse. These colors reflected on our faces as we stared, slack-jawed, at the power of that sky—stunning like a pop-up picture book, mesmerizing, vital, and more intriguing than the land. Mt. Charleston, in profile, was like Mt. Fuji in triplicate to the tenth power, on steroids. The sunsets, the sunsets, the sunsets. Grand in the grandest sense of that word. Nothing anywhere could ever be as breathtaking as those sunsets. Who could breathe when the sky lit up this way? It seemed as though we lived in heaven when it became so much more than blue and vast. This was the time when I believed that God was in the heavens, smiling, directing this beauty, this pageant, this wondrous scene before my eyes. This was when I felt blessed to be human, to be part of all of this.

The irony is that the desert has captivated me. This bony terrain, this lonely yet wise place, teaching what it is to be left on one's own, subject to wind and sand blowing against one's face. Insulting. Isolating. Vast. A piece in the puzzle of eternity. It is a stretch of geography that explains God, heaven, and hell with no words, no scriptures, no ideologies. This wind has blown away all of my answers after years of considering various and sundry ideas. I'm almost a clean sweep. Just like the desert on a windy day. An empty cow skull on land stretched across the earth's surface. A drum skin unattached to a drum.

The desert. By all accounts, I seem to be its captive, continually drawn back to this skeletal land, to the long distances with no inhabitants except the grassless mountains, an occasional bighorn sheep, the red rock and sand, which are altered by the flash floods charging through the gullies, and the acres and acres of repetitive shrubs. I'm glad that some places such as the Lake Mead National Recreation Area have been preserved to remind us of this spaciousness, this expanse, this empty and daunting creation. I am dismayed when I see how the valleys are being filled by thousands, millions, living in sand-colored apartments, attending beige churches, sleeping in caramel houses dropped into the sand by a developer with big bucks in mind, and some living in homes built to look like medieval castles with doors too tall and strong for actual use. It's all staging: "Yes, I live in a castle. See? I'm King of the Desert. King or Queen of Something."

And palm trees. There weren't any when I was growing up, and now, they're everywhere, gracing the streets and the boulevards, making the desert more hospitable.

The desert always lies in wait, clucking its dry tongue at anybody's whimsical sense of propriety. It frames the existence and borders of lives there, this blatant, don't-mess-with-me desert with its horned toads, scorpions, rattlesnakes, deep and blowing sand, sage, creosote, and teddy bear cholla. When the wind stops blowing and the hand of providence holds me close and I return to discover the reason why the desert has such a hold on me, I can see it is a quiet, subtle, magical place with its cobbled pavement, its darkly stained desert varnish, its hard pebble faces polished by wind-driven sand. It is a place designed by large hands: alluvial fans spread by flowing water from the mouths of canyons, the spread of gravel by flash floods, large and small pieces of volcanic eruptions called lava. It is ubiquitous, proud, haughty, even hostile, though it responds when I don't expect it to be something other than it is. There is that moment when the sage gives up its scent to the rain, when the paper-thin globe mallow teaches me what vulnerability looks like. Its scaly survivors leave tracks. Whispery. Barely discernable. I can learn something from their darting skills.

When the wind takes time to rest, there is silence. An elongated quiet. An aloneness. This tells me that, against all odds, certain things last. There are the occasional shouts of yucca blossoming, garish slips of Indian sagebrush, and short appearances by one-day bloomers, but, overall, the land is shy and subtle and speaks to those who take their time to wait for its face to show. Why are we all so impatient? Why do we make up answers to give us comfort rather than listen to the land, which has so much to tell us? The land has been here much longer than any of us ever will be, and it is alive. It is speaking if only we could listen.

I don't say much these days—desert dry, shy, or aware I don't know much of anything, who knows—nor do I try to assert my know-it-all personality anymore. Spoken words blew away one day. I watch the position of the sun in the sky—how it rises at dawn and sinks at day's end. How the sky illuminates into something I can't gather into small thoughts. If I had my druthers, I would be the wind or the sand, blowing every which way, settling, then unsettling. Maybe that is the truth of it anyway.

Part Two

BEYOND THE DESERT

THE KNIFE HANDLER

Vernon, "I'm Weighing My Options," has straight pencil-sketch lips that rarely curve at the edges. He wears his soft felt hat at right angles and moves with his head plumbline straight with the rest of his spine. He's also a man of some reputation—the basketmaking teacher at the Ozark Folk Center and a master with the edge of a knife. I'm trying to add a new place to my repertoire, desert dweller that I am. I'm also Vernon's student, constructing a white oak basket for which I'm suffering greatly: after four days of whittling, my wrists are burning. I can barely lift the knife anymore.

He and I are driving together in his ancient Dodge truck while my three boys are back at the motel in Mountain View, my fourteen-year-old playing watchdog over the TV remote and his younger brothers (we support each other's impulses). Vernon has narrow bones in his face, eyes like pale blue marbles, and hands mean with the knife. (*Mean* means *good* right now, don't let me mislead you. I pick up local color like a chameleon.) I'm not at Vernon's mercy or anything like that, except my breathing's shallow. My lungs are hurting. I'm thinking I've gambled one too many times.

Last Monday after class, Vernon peeked in while I was play-ing the "Moonlight Sonata" on the piano in a small side room at the Center. He'd stood in the doorway, listening. I saw him. I lifted my hands off the keys. "I love piano playing," he said, com-ing closer, and we talked about music, then drifted into the topic of old-time religion. He told me I should come visit his church "just a ways off."

Now we're driving into twilight and the deep dark woods, thick with white oak and shortleaf pine, to who knows what and who knows where, some place he calls New Nata, and I'm think-ing for all the world I'm a fool who's left her boys behind and who might get jumped or kidnapped or waylaid by crazy moon-shiners or big bears. Or even Vernon.

But come on now. There's something about Vernon that's right to the toe-square. Maybe I'm too curious, but I did decide to take my chances. I'd driven to his house, our prearranged meeting place at the prearranged time. But why in heaven's name had I climbed into this rumply Dodge truck with too many dents in one fender? Soda-pop stains shine off the dashboard. A scratchy radio plays local bluegrass. Keeping the beat, Vernon dips his stiff chin into the air in front of his poked-out Adam's apple.

My sons and I are spending a couple of weeks at Mountain View while my husband is a guest professor in the law school at the University of Arkansas in Fayetteville. I've decided it's important for all of us to know more than the harsh beauty of the desert where we live and the vistas and valleys of the Great Basin where we drive every summer to visit our relatives. I hoped to steep our three sons in Ozarkness—the thick forests and slow-moving rivers plus classes in fiddling (middle son, Jeremy, a wizard on the violin), bluegrass music (oldest son, Chris, hot on the guitar), whittling, broom-making, whatever they were interested in, though Brad's too young to be interested in any-thing more than the fishing pond. In addition, I'd find time for a basketmaking class in which we chopped down a tree—a slim river birch—shucked off the shiny bark, and cut strips of wood to use in our baskets-to-be. My wrists ache. As Vernon's turning onto another narrow road and we're cruising further into the holler, I feel jabs of lightning in that little old wrist of mine that holds my right hand in place. I'm a tall girl with small bones, except in the hips, of course. My hips were made for birthing but my wrists are delicate.

About half an hour ago, I braked in front of Vernon's house, stretched my arms, and wondered what I'd find inside this low-lying, cinder-block house with dark-brown curtains in the windows. I unlatched my car door and unfolded my tired pony legs. I stood tall on hard dirt, stretched again, and then took cautious steps toward Vernon's. Some eyes might be watching, I thought as I sidestepped some puddles. Someone could be assessing this Mormon girl from Salt Lake City, this big-city girl from the West. I sighed relief when a dumpling of a woman answered the door. Greeting me with a tired smile, her blue-checked apron tied high around her waist, she said she was Ella, wouldn't I come in, she and her husband were expecting me.

Vernon appeared out of the misty-moisty kitchen, sleeves rolled up and an embroidered potato-sack dishtowel in his hands. It had seen some days—coffee stains, burnt grease, holes in the cloth. His wife excused herself, saying she had to look after water boiling around the lids of her Mason jars. "Snap beans." She smiled with pleasure, as if snap beans were the essence of life.

"Sit you down, girl," Vernon said. I took a seat on a sofa that had seen a few too many bottoms in its time. The springs protested as I sank into the cushion. I wondered if I'd ever be able to stand back up.

In class, after my wrist gave out, I watched Vernon, who could do more with wood than anyone I'd ever met, treat my portion of tree trunk as if it were a cold slab of lard. Without rulers or measuring tapes, he stripped pieces for my basket, the same length, the same width, time after time. No rehearsing. No false starts or nicks in the damp insides of the trunk. Then he whittled my basket handle, all the time whistling, sometimes singing a few lines from songs I'd never heard. And after class, when he overheard me playing those few bars of "Moonlight" on an old-time piano I'd asked permission to play, that's what got us started with all of this. "Music is my blood," I told him. "And I'm curious about people and their worship—how religious people think they're getting to the other side they talk about and what they do to hook up with Spirit—that something that keeps us all wondering."

Now he was walking to a cabinet where an old Victrola held its curvy head like a proud goose on top of the cupboard, the one he was opening.

"I've got something here," he said, shuffling through a neat stack of pamphlets, sheet music, and loose papers. "I've been thinking you need to know about this." He grabbed two thin paper-covered books from the cabinet and sat next to me. The sofa sank even lower.

"Shape notes," he said. "You ever heard of shape notes?"

"Can't say that I have," I answered, watching him open a small book called *Joy in Singing, 135 New and Favorite Gospel Songs for Group Singing, Singing Schools and Singing Conventions*. At the bottom of the first page, I read it was published by Jack Taylor and the Stamps-Baxter Editorial Staff of Stamps-Baxter Music of the Zondervan Corporation out of Dallas. Bible Belt stuff. First song: "Jesus Is Coming Again."

"Look at these shapes," he said, as excited as if he were showing me the shores of a newly discovered land.

The notes weren't round, as I was used to seeing on a staff. "How does this work?"

"Simple do, re, mi," he said. "You can use this system in any key. The 'do' is always a triangle, 're' is a half moon, 'mi' is a diamond."

I found a "fa," which looked like the upper half of a square box cut on the diagonal, "sol," which was the kind of round note I was used to seeing, "la" was a pure square, and "ti" a diamond with a rounded top, the diamond-ring variety.

"Wow," I said, the easy word I used when nothing more descriptive popped up. I leafed through the book, wanting to sight-read through some of these hymns like "I Want to Be More Like Him Every Day," "Keep the Prayer Line Open," and "Jesus is the Friend of Sinners." The shape notes were arranged the way any round notes would be on the familiar musical staff, so it wasn't hard to read the melody line and hum softly to myself. I was in Southern Baptist land though I didn't know the differences between First and Second and Calvary Baptist and whatever other names I'd seen on signs in front of tall-skinny, small-chunky, and house-of-many-mansions churches labeled Baptist.

"That book's for you," Vernon said, handing me a second one. "Both of 'em."

This was new territory, these shape notes, these black diamonds, triangles, and squares in these hills in the holler. They were something totally alien and unknown to me, even with all my music training and vaunted college degree.

"We best be getting on to church," Vernon said, springing quickly from the sagging cushions. "I'll be happy to drive you there. We don't need two cars."

"Maybe I should drive my own car?"

"No, no. My truck knows the ruts on the road to New Nata."

"Well, is Ella coming with us?" I asked, using the sofa's arm to steady myself back onto my feet and peering into the kitchen at the woman lifting the lid of a deep-water cooker to release a cloud of steam.

"No. She has to wait out those beans and make sure they're sealed tight."

My hands limped out at the sides of my legs.

It's not that I didn't trust Vernon. He seemed straight,

through and through. A man of his word. A man who knew how to rub strips of white oak silky smooth with the back of his knife. After all, he'd salvaged the strips of my basket when my wrist gave out. He was a man who loved music. Yet I'd hesitated as I'd slid onto the cracked vinyl seat cover, closed the passenger door, and heard the truck's engine roar.

Now, the headlights are slashing branches and tree trunks in the dimming light. I've seen *Deliverance* and read "A Good Man is Hard to Find" by Flannery O'Connor, where the family rides recklessly to their end. I'm thinking of my three boys tucked back in the motel, husband back in Fayetteville teaching law classes, while I'm out here on a bumpy road going deeper and deeper into the hills. The light is fading fast—in fact, who's kidding who, the light is gone except for a silver-gray lining on the horizon. The pinks and oranges have sunk away. The beam from Vernon's headlights bounces high and low as the road twists and turns. The skeleton branches reach out across the road from time to time, nothing at windshield level, but close enough to scrape the top of the truck.

"Not far," Vernon says. His lips pressed tight, he holds his head up high to peer over the dashboard, past the smeared windshield, out into the darkness where rabbits or racoons might be making frenzied runs across the road. Chuckholes. Washboard ripples occasionally. It's too late for me to run. My instincts are usually good. Usually.

Just when we've rounded one too many curves and I think I should tell Vernon thanks but no thanks, I don't have time for this and I wasn't ready to be gone this long, a tiny church appears, white in the graying gloom, windows yellow with light. There's a high-ridged roof, dark shingles, a no-account setting for a church, buried in the woods as it is, but maybe that's only because I don't understand backroads. Vernon seems to know exactly where he's going as he squeezes into the middle of assorted trucks, Fords and Chevys parked at cock-eyed angles.

I slide out of the cab. Vernon and I walk side-by-side through an open door, me analyzing the narrowness of the chapel and the pews on either side that hold no more than seven bodies apiece. No crosses or statuary anywhere, just a pulpit, a few chairs on the dais, a spinet of a piano that looks battered and out of tune, untrustworthy and beaten into submission from years of hands playing the black keys with tucked and rolled fists.

Vernon introduces me to the first person we encounter, a sleepy-eyed woman in a comfortable jersey with white dots, who tilts her head low, though there's nothing lost to her down-looking eyes.

"Welcome," she pronounces the word softly, without the *L*, pulling on the little finger of her left hand like it was one of those Chinese straw torture devices.

"She plays the piano good," Vernon says proudly, as if that were a rare gift automatically vaulting me onto a pedestal. Then he turns to me in a slightly stiff way, almost as if he's made out of wood himself. "You'll play the piano for the choir tonight, won't you?"

"I couldn't do that," I say before thinking about it, wishing I could bend over and pull up invisible socks that have fallen down in response to his invitation, wishing I'd stop breathing in such a shallow way, trying to put this whole scenario together in my head. I'm a woman who's studied classical masterpieces. I practice endlessly. I'm precise. "I don't know your music," I say, remembering the songs in the shape-note singing books, nothing I'd ever seen or heard before.

"But you can play, can't you?" Vernon insists, his pale blue eyes shocked that I'd resist his request. "You know the notes."

"Sure," I say, "but not this kind of music. This style," I stutter.

"What do you mean, *this* kind of music?" he says, his whittling hands tight on his hips. "Music is music."

"But . . ." I say, realizing that nothing I say will make any sense here. "This is all new to me."

"God's in the music—when we sing, we shout. It's not about doing it right."

I swallow big-time. Besides being a perfectionist, I can be shy.

"Well, then," he insists when I don't respond, "you'll lead the choir, won't you?"

The lights in the ceiling feel hot and steamy, like they're glaring spotlights on a stage already well-lit. My blouse is moist under the arms and at the neck. I think about the door. I'm one of the deer people hunt in these hills. The hunter's pointing his arrow, and I can't escape whichever way I move.

Two wiry men in overalls walk through the door and touch their hats to greet Vernon. "Evenin'," one says. A couple come through the door arm-in-arm, patting each other's elbows, black broad-heeled shoes on the woman, summer-mudded boots on the man. Women in paisleys and swirling stripes, in lace-necked blouses, speckled splotches of color on cotton and jersey dresses swishing through the door, finding a place in the pews, wriggling into comfort on broad and narrow buttocks. The congregation gathers and sits and murmurs, a few eyes in my direction.

Vernon sits in the first pew, pats the place next to him, and I sit while the minister greets everyone—black smooth hair, long white cheeks, eyebrows rising to a point at each end, all this above a well-worn and shiny dark-blue suit, dark-blue knit tie. "Wecome," he says. "We're gathered here in worship to thank our Lord, Jesus Christ. I say Jesus, yes Jesus."

"Amen," a woman in the congregation answers back.

Yes, I say to myself, nodding my head yes to the brothers and sisters gathered here. They're hoping for that connection to Spirit that can pierce their chests, sitting as they are in the pews of this pointy-roofed church in the middle of the Ozarks.

"Yes, dear God," I pray to myself, remembering what I'm about to do. "Help me with this choir. Fill the music with thy Spirit. Please and amen."

"Our choir will now sing for us," the minister says, and a group of ten or eleven people gathers at the far side of the platform.

"Come on," Vernon says, handing me a hymnal, then standing to make his way to join the choir. He stops briefly to make an announcement to the people in the pews. "This here lady is from the Ozark Center class. She knows music." In an aside, he tells me to open the hymn book to number 51: "Little Is Much When God Is In It."

I face this group of curious onlookers, each of us assessing and peering across borders to see what lies there. I open the little book in my hand. I smile at the blur of people—blues, reds, yellows, the primary colors, 1-2-3. A few noses and eyeglasses here and there. Jump, I tell myself. I imagine there's a piano playing, giving the choir an introduction, but I feel as though I've already jumped into an abyss.

I raise both arms. This is what I've done when I've led the congregation in hymn-singing in Salt Lake City. I look into the faces of these strangers on this wide variety of bodies, then raise one arm higher to signal the upbeat: 1-2-3-ahhhp. But the signal doesn't work here. There's no sound. They all look at me in expectation, believing and trusting because they've been told I know music. If I give in to my anxiety, I'll drown right in front of everybody. I'll embarrass Vernon and myself. The only way out . . . Try again.

Where I get the courage I'll never know, but I try the upbeat again and add my voice. "In the harvest field now ripened," I sing thinly. The diamonds and squares and triangles jump all over the page, but I still know where a G sits on the music staff, and then an F and a B flat. I hold steady, the familiar five parallel lines to guide me. I gain in volume and clarity. Yes! I can hear their voices. Hallelujah. "Labor not for wealth or fame. There's a crown and you can win it if you go in Jesus' name."

Four verses. Four choruses. "We'll be happy, glad, and free"—the last line of the fourth verse. Everyone has gotten into

this. Their faces are uplifted; their voices sound out all the way
from their toes. We've come together in that harmonious connection that sometimes happens with music, that moment when
all the voices are more than all the singers, that rare, beautiful
thing. And during that instant between the end of the song and
the reemergence of real time, I feel like spreading my arms out
wide and wider and almost bursting with the feeling of fresh air
in my lungs.

A few of the choir rock their heads in approval, their eyes
closed. They don't look at me or each other. They're caught in
something bigger. Some of them lumber back to their pews
without any sign of response; others step lightly on the pine
floor, happy to be alive. There's the sound of big and little shoes
finding a comfortable place to rest, a few coughs, a few purses
clicking shut.

I touch Vernon's arm as we return to our front-row pew, just
lightly, and his ear lobes turn pink. I'm not sure who lives inside
of Vernon or if I've crossed some boundary I shouldn't have,
but I appreciate it when he turns and grants me a stiff, satisfied
smile. It's not just that his discovery at the Ozark Folk Center
hasn't let him down, which is the gratitude I'm feeling. It's as
if he knew what would happen before it happened, as if he has
no conception of anyone who loves music doing anything other
than making music of whatever kind. Vernon believes that God's
in the bones of music. God gave it to us. To sing. To play. To let
rise up however it will.

I'm moved by this simplicity.

My mind twists and turns, paralysis by analysis. I've worked
hard to figure it all out—this business of whether or not there's
a God in the first place, whether the Divine is masculine or
feminine, how humans serve a higher purpose. Dependence vs.
independence. Surrender vs. fight. And then there's that thing
about people being godly and yet stiff in their ways until their
goodness turns sour and blind certainty enters in. The Divine is

unknowable, but I want to know what it means to surrender—
whether or not that means lying flat on the hard-pack country
road and letting a Dodge Ram roll over me. I've thought about
all of this. I'm trying to listen. But it seems there are too many
voices calling out: this is the way, the truth, the light. Listen to
me, listen to me. I've cornered The Truth. I've caged it. If you'll
only listen to me, to me, to me, to us, to us, to us."

As I sit in the first row in the first pew in this chapel in New
Nata, Arkansas, my hands grip my knees in an attempt to keep
them from tensing into nervous claws. I'm thinking again about
my boys who are so good to put up with me and encourage me to
follow my crazy impulses. But I need to do better by them. Only
crazy women would leave their children in a motel in Arkansas
by themselves even if they're old enough to manage. I'm such a
fool. I should be trampled or hung.

With no other choice but to sit here and let my shame burn
over, I turn my attention back to the preacher. He's well spoken. He's worked the hell-fire-and-damnation sermon to a fine
art. His voice is rising. The air's filling with his pleading, with
the urgency of his sermon reprimanding us sinners who squirm
uncomfortably on these hard pews, our sins flashing through
our minds. Beneath a three-armed brass chandelier whose low-
watt bulb's glowing, he's asking us to surrender, to say, "I give up.
Save me. Save me, now."

"Is there anyone," he asks, looking slowly at each member of
the congregation, "who's being told by Spirit to come to the front
and be saved? I know there's someone out there. It could be you."
He's working up a sweat. A strand of his smooth black hair has
fallen into his eye. He loosens his tie. "Do you hear Jesus talking
to you? Do you feel that fire telling you to be saved before it's too
late?"

I'm feeling inadequate as a mother and a decent human
being. I'm suggestible and therefore not impervious to his questions. This guy's on fire. I fight with my hands to keep them in

place on the flat of my thighs. I spread out the material of my skirt, smoothing it, undoing bulges. I fold my arms, unfold them again. It's like something's working its fingers underneath my backside and trying to get me to stand up and rush to the front of this chapel, to declare my inadequacies before this congregation and this preacher, to ask to be saved.

The preacher is eyeballing the congregation. He is waiting. His eyes pass over me, then come back to check. I could swoon, though I won't. I'm precise. I'm in control. I won't gush, fall on my knees, and be overcome by fervor. I lower my head and relax my hands over the ends of my knees. I breathe deeply. I will stay sensible.

My moment passes as so many other moments have passed when I've paused in front of a decision—when I've used my head and remembered to be realistic. This is beneath me, this business of being saved and throwing one's self publicly into the arms of an exhorter. People don't just throw themselves. They're supposed to be rational and sure about such a big decision.

Suddenly, a young boy in a yellow sweater vest bumbles from a pew and stumbles in his black and white Oxfords that seem too big for him toward the front, the pulpit, the preacher. His mother leans out over the edge of her row to follow her mighty offspring with her teary, proud eyes. The preacher holds out his arms. He has someone to save. He's done what he's been called to do. He puts his long-fingered hands on the shoulders of this young champion who's come forward, this young warrior for The Right. He gathers as much as he can of the boy in the palms of his hands and squeezes with pride.

"Wecome, my son," he says, his voice trembling, his suit coat fanned to the side while he tugs his pants back to waist level. "Jesus is your Savior, boy. He will protect you, young John Baker. Do you feel the love of God pouring onto your head right now? Do you know you're saved from this moment on?"

John Baker could be caught up in what he thinks he's

supposed to do and what might make his mother happy, yet his face shines as he looks up at his minister, a big smile sprinkled with freckles.

There's clapping as the preacher and the boy grip hands and raise them like a referee does with the winner in a boxing ring. There's noise all around as people stand to applaud this young man who has chosen well. With a slight turn of my head and strained peripheral vision, I witness shiny lines of moisture on some cheeks, though I don't dare turn full around to look in their faces on the chance they might look back at mine. I'm not sure what's written there at this moment.

I check on Vernon, the man with no apparent emotion on his face or in the set of his body. His arms are folded to the square—firm and resolute. His knees are bent at right angles and his feet rest parallel on the scuffed floor. Yet, I've seen him with wood. He can talk to it, feel its give and take, and convince it to bend to the will of his knife. It becomes supple and coopera-tive in the hands of this master who sits next to me, working his lower jaw slightly. I sit back against the pew and gather myself into the pose of a casual observer.

With one hand resting on the boy's head, the preacher says, "We'll have John's baptism this Saturday. Ya'll come and praise the Lord for this fine young man. Give it up out there for John Baker." Then he affectionately musses John's hair.

John smiles a crooked smile, bashful, then bows his head to the side as he walks back toward his mother, stumbling every third step on the shoelaces of his oxfords. The slicked-back do his mother must have styled for this meeting is now bent to one side, and yet he's still smiling, ready to take on all of creation.

"And I'm hoping you'll all follow young John's example," the preacher is saying when I tune back into the meeting. "There's a tent revival this coming weekend over at Desha. We should all make an effort to be there. Preacher White is visiting from Heber Springs and has a lot to tell us about. Maybe the rest of you laggards will take on the Lord Jesus for him if you won't for me. Don't wait, all of you. The time is drawing nigh."

For a fleeting moment, I'm wondering if I shouldn't consider this revival, showing up in a Levi skirt and a homespun blouse. Maybe I'm unyielding and too tight for my own good. Maybe I'm stuck in thinking I have all the answers. Maybe I don't understand the first thing about Jesus—who he is and how he saves.

I wonder if Vernon is considering taking Ella with him if she's finished with her canning. How does he feel about all of this? I notice his bright pink cheeks on his shock-white face, his eyes filled with slivers of sky and his jaw set. I wonder if he's been saved on an evening such as this. I wonder if he's walked up that aisle to bare his soul to the preacher and the congregation, if he's offered his heart to be pierced by the arrow of light, though that image seems closer to the Catholics than the Baptists. On the surface he seems so tight, like he lives inside the fortress of his well-ordered, even rote mechanism. Does he ever let down his guard?

Except, the afternoon he'd found me playing the piano in a side room at the Center, Vernon brought in a flat, supple board about a yard long in the shape of a figure eight with a wide waist. He also brought a jointed doll with hinged arms and legs, a round Gingerbread-man face and a hole in its back into which he'd screwed a long stick. Vernon sat on one end of the board while the other end hung out over the edge of his chair. Then he held the doll out over the board and tapped it in time to my music. The doll's arms and legs flailed and flapped and made me laugh. It had a flirtatious look in its eye.

"This here's a dancing doll," he'd said with pride.

"Oh, can I try it out? My boys would love this." I sat on one end of the board and took the stick in hand, the doll full of personality dangling on the other end. As I tapped the board, it began to dance, one arm circling full around. "Where can I get one of these?" I asked, excited, the ready purchaser of goods, the eternal shopper.

"Right here in the gift shop," he said. "Packaged for sale."

But now as we're listening to the preacher wrap up his sermon, it occurs to me that I hadn't thought to inquire whether Vernon had made the doll. If he had, he'd probably been bursting buttons to tell me this was something he'd whittled. Maybe because he thought I knew music and how creative people always want to show off their stuff, he hoped I'd take an interest in his talent. But I hadn't thought to ask. I'd accepted his wooden façade and stiff-lipped ways as I'd said goodbye to him and gone off to the gift shop to buy one of those dolls. I wonder if my boys are playing with it right now in Mountain View. My boys. I miss my boys. Oh, I hope everything is all right.

"I better get back," I tell Vernon after the preacher says his Amen. "My sons will be waiting for me."

"Nice of you to come," Vernon says as he stands, his chest tight like he wants to make sure nothing falls out. He nods his head to a few people, I listen to the woman with sleepy eyes, "Thanking you, Ma'am," and watch a small smile creep onto her lips. Then we breast the cool night air, trucks revving their motors, beefy coupes rolling carefully back toward their homes, a few voices floating across the place where cars had been parked during those few moments out of time. Maybe that's what it's all about: being out of time, listening for voices we can't quite hear, all of us suspecting there's something that explains this concoction called life.

We're quiet as we bump back to the highway, where my car waits and where, on down the road, my boys wait. I'm no longer spooked by the road-brushing tree branches of the wide-as-they-are-tall white oaks that scrape the top of the truck's cab. We're both full of contemplation and not in the mood for small talk. Vernon peers over the dashboard, watching for white-tailed deer and other critters of the night and for ruts that could scrape his oil pan.

As we bump and jar and jostle, I hang onto the dashboard

to keep from crashing my hip bone into the door or crush-sliding into Vernon. The only thing I know for sure is that Vernon loves music and making things out of wood. I have a basket he put the finishing touches on that I wouldn't sell for a thousand dollars, not after all those hours of cramping my fingers. I saw how he loved making the doll dance and whirl its arms like a tap dancer at the Bijou—the doll he'd probably whittled to life. A whittler. A knife handler. That's what Vernon is. I think about the edge of a knife and how it can cut, slash and wound, and yet, how it can coax a face from the insides of a stick—its single edge a double edge. In that way it reminds me of music running inside Vernon and me, filling each of us, eroding our hard hearts and rigid minds, the things we think we are, the things we think others are.

We make a right turn onto the paved highway, back in real time again, and before I know it, I've said goodbye and I'm behind the wheel of my car, hot-footing it back to Mountain View while a fiddle tune on a tape I bought at the Center rises out the open windows into the night and into the rippling leaves of passing trees.

Dancing With The Sacred

PART ONE: 1985

This morning after my three teenage sons have bolted out the side door, late for school, scraping their backpacks against the door frame, which is already scarred, I look at the piles of breakfast dishes. Specks of yesterday's cake mix, having been flipped from the wire arms of the electric beater, remain on the kitchen window above the sink. I open the refrigerator and notice a puddle of sticky grape juice marring the shine of the glass shelf. Closing the white-enameled door covered with magnets, I leave this messy kitchen, this reminder of my ineptitude, which will depress me even more if I think about it much longer.

I need to talk to someone. But who wants to listen? Who would I tell anyway? Maybe I should get on my knees and talk to the heavens but I need to move more than I need to stay still. I need to feel my body alive—my arms stretching up and out, my blood speeding through my veins. Mid-step in the front hall where family and visitors come and go, I'm struck with an idea.

I turn the corner to the family room. It's filled with furniture, but because I feel compelled to dance, I push the wing chair to the wall. The sofa as well. Now there's enough space, and it feels as though, instead of praying, I could dance with God somehow, the Divine could take me in Its arms. Today. Right now. I still believe in God. In a divine presence. In something bigger than I am.

I thumb through my stack of albums until I find Prokofiev's "Concerto No. 1 for Piano & Orchestra, Op. 10," lift the record out of the sleeve, and set it on the turntable. Aiming the needle, I find the first groove and wait for the ebb and flow of the orchestra, the in and out. The three beginning chords cause my arms to pimple with goose flesh. I take two steps to the middle of the room and raise my arms in a circle, fingertips touching. Slowly at first, I move, one foot pointed to the right as if I were the most elegant ballerina in the most satin of toe shoes. My right leg lifts poetically, delicately for such a long leg. The other knee bends in a demi-plié. But the music swarms inside and splits into the tributaries of my veins and vessels and becomes blood. Things become more primitive. I stamp the pressing beat into the floor. I bend to one side, my arms swimming. I'm a willow, a genie escaping the bottle, the wind, the sun. I'm light. The magic carpet of music carries me places where I can escape—to the Maasai Mara where bare legs of dancers reflect the light of a campfire and beaded hoops circle their necks or to the Greek islands with their red-roofed white houses stark against the cobalt blue sky and water. The music lifts me out of this minute, this hour, this day. I'm dancing to the opening and closing of the heart valves, to the beat of humanity, giving my all to the air, giving it up to the room. Whirling. Bending. Leaping. Twisting. Twirling and twirling to the beat. Getting close to what God is.

The chords build to a climax until there is no more building possible. The release comes. The final chord. The finale. The sound dies away, as if it had never been there. The room still swirls, passing me by even as I stand still, panting, trying to return my breathing to normal once again. I'm dizzy. I steady

myself in the middle of the Persian rug and wonder why Prokofiev had to write an end to this concerto. The needle ticks on the
record in the black space left on the vinyl. I stand quietly until
the room stops with me, until the sense of having traveled elsewhere fades away.

I look at this sky-blue family room in our home in Salt Lake
City where David and I are raising our children—the family
pictures on the wall, the framed copy of David's and my college graduation diplomas, the Persian carpet with its blue stain
where our son Christopher spilled a bucket of blue paint when
he was two. My eyes linger at the sandstone hearth where our
son Brad fell one time and split open his head, which had to be
stitched together in the emergency room. Then my eyes brush
past the bookcase with its many volumes of books, psychological tomes, scriptures, all of which are supposed to have answers.
The leather wing chair that has been peppered with the points
of darts thrown when I, Mother, wasn't looking and before I,
Mother, hid the darts in a secret place. The wooden floor, which
I'm supposed to polish once a week with a flat mop and its terry-
cloth cover. I, the Mother, stand here looking at the things which
verify my place in the world and also at the evidence that I hav-
en't always been watchful at the helm—I, the Mother who is supposed to make the world all right for her husband and children.
I, the heart of the home, the protector, the nurturer. I should
dance again, turn the music up before my mind chases me into
that place where I feel badly about myself.

I learned dancing from my father, who loved to polka when
Lawrence Welk's orchestra played on television, and at dance
festivals sponsored by my church when I was a teenager. We
danced the cha-cha, tango, and Viennese waltz. At age twenty-
one, I danced myself into a Mormon temple marriage and made
promises to help build the Kingdom of God here on earth. I
gave birth to four sons whom I dressed each Sunday for church
meetings. I tried to be a good wife. I canned pears and ground

wheat for bread, I taught Relief Society lessons and accompanied singers and violinists on the piano, I bore testimony to the truthfulness of the gospel countless numbers of times. Yet dancing seems to be my real home—the place where I can feel the Divine enlarging my heart, this dancing.

○

Last night as I twisted and turned in bed with my newfound knowledge that there are other women in David's life and with the realization that things are changing in my marriage, which I thought would always be there, I felt tempted to jump out of bed, open the blinds, and search the night sky for the letter of the law burnished among the stars—a big, pulsing neon sign that said, "Thou Shalt Not Endure to the End." Except that's all I know how to do: persist, endure, keep dancing. Things have to work out, don't they?

Mormons are taught not only to endure to the end, but to persist in the process of perfecting themselves: "As man is now, God once was; As God is now, man may be." Lorenzo Snow, fifth president of the Church, wrote the couplet after he heard Joseph Smith's lecture on this doctrine. I've tried for perfection, but I haven't thought that word through to its logical conclusion. I haven't wondered enough about who is the arbiter of perfection.

"Perfection," Webster's says: "Freedom from fault or defect." Is that even possible? Perfection is a nice idea, but that definition makes the idea of becoming like God stifling. It's tied to shoulds, oughts, and knots that bind, rather than releasing one to live a full life and to dance the dance. Even Brigham Young said, "Let us not narrow ourselves up." Trying to be perfect, when the world and David have no intention of complying with my notions of perfection, is killing me.

The telephone rings. I don't want to leave this room just yet. I want to bring back the music, to keep God here with me, even if He has places to go, things to do, and I, too, have my responsibilities. But if God is my Father, as I've been taught, then I am his daughter. I need to trust that He'll always be with me somehow, that there will be a next dance.

Ignoring the phone, I think of something William James said in *The Varieties of Religious Experience* about how a prophet can seem a lonely madman.

> If his doctrine proves contagious enough to spread to any others, it becomes a definite . . . heresy. But if it then still proves contagious enough to triumph over persecution, it becomes itself an orthodoxy; and when a religion has become an orthodoxy, its day of inwardness is over: the spring is dry; the faithful live at second hand exclusively . . . in spite of whatever goodness [the new church] may foster, [it] can be counted on as a staunch ally in every attempt to stifle the . . . bubblings of the fountain from which in purer days it drew its own supply of inspiration.

I suspect I'm caught in the web of orthodoxy, that I'm inflexible and that my spring is dry. I'm living secondhand, unwilling to consider any other options to my parents' teachings and my Mormon upbringing. But I don't feel inflexible when I dance. I'm the fountain, even the source of this fountain—the water. Raising both arms to the ceiling, I'm hoping I can stretch into the heavens. "I am with you," I hear God whisper.

Daylight pours through the windows, exchanging the light in this room for that of the day. My hands press flat against each other in front of my heart. "Thanks for the dance," I whisper. "Thank you," I think I hear a whisper back.

The telephone has stopped ringing. A floorboard creaks beneath my foot. I can hear the refrigerator humming down the hall. Commerce and industry, motherhood and wifehood with all of their demands calling again.

PART TWO: 1991

One particular Bedouin man catches my attention. He's carrying plates away from our feast, preparing for after-dinner entertainment: *Omar Sharif*, I think to myself. What else would a first-time-in-Jordan, US citizen think, with those molten eyes and their hint of "take me to the Casbah"? Of course, this is my movie-acquired understanding of a man like this one. He could be a thousand things, maybe a Muslim appearing for tourists to make ends meet, to feed his children, or he could be, plain and simply, a Bedouin, a wanderer. But it's useless to care about definitions this evening as we're gathered in this tent, two small groups of tourists wanting a glimpse into the mysterious life of a Bedouin (for a slight fee, of course).

One week before this night, my husband David and I had sailed down the Nile to Luxor, flown to Abu Simbel to view the gargantuan pharaohs carved into stone, hiked Mt. Sinai before sunrise and reveled in the purple fog bubbling out of mountain crevices far below—a perfect setting for Moses and his tablets, no doubt. While traveling by bus through the rest of the Sinai Desert, one woman in our tour group—a victim of the dreaded tourist's gambu—bolted for the door to be let outside for privacy. While we waited, the rest of us caught sight of something moving toward us on the stark horizon. It looked like the rising of three small ships from the sea. Everyone made their guesses until we could definitely see three Bedouin people, their heads wrapped in scarves, their feet covered in soft leather, riding camels toward us.

One musician tunes his oud—the bulbous-backed Middle Eastern guitar—and another warms the reed on his oboe-like instrument, the nay. *Has he charmed reptiles as well as humans? My blood rises in anticipation of music, sweet music. Maybe there'll be dancing.*

Several of us climbed off the bus that day, me with a packet of pencils in hand. One Bedouin man asked if we needed any help. We said no, we'd be fine. I handed him the pencils. "For your children." He swooped low from his seat on the camel's hump, his hand touching mine. I wanted to stay in the thrill of that moment: surrounded by the haughty faces of the camels, to hold on to some kind of thread that could keep me connected to this world of which I knew nothing at all. But the bus driver said, "Time to go." We said our thank yous and goodbyes and drove off to the shores of the Red Sea, the Gulf of Aqaba our front door.

The next morning, barefoot in sand, I gave a dancing lesson to the six women-of-all-sizes of our group. They'd heard me talking about being a devotee of Middle Eastern dance and how I loved the idea of moving like a W-O-M-A-N instead of the unconscious maiden. Shoeless and willing, the women made figure eights with their hips, snaked their arms, and twirled the scarves lent to them until each billowed like the sail of a ship in sea breeze. Caught in this woman magic, we were all convinced that we should perform for our husbands and lovers and that each of them needed to make a trip to the bazaar for jingling coin belts, necklaces, finger cymbals, and gauzy scarves of their own.

Our performance that night, complete with our two Muslim guides peeking through the splits of palm fronds, was short and sweet. We made a dramatic entrance, clanked our budget finger cymbals, and attempted the same step/thrust-hip move all at the same time. Then each woman took her turn at stardom on the shores of the Red Sea. But because one lost her composure and giggled, the rest couldn't maintain the seductive illusion. All six of us dissolved into bent-over laughter. Afterward, everyone in a glorious party mood, we strolled the beach where light from a crescent moon striped the water and a velvet breeze caressed our skin. Each couple returned to their cabaña in the settling darkness.

David and I walked through the open door, the interior space sterile after the silky night and the laughter. Silence opened its mouth. We entered. We'd said too much to each other during our thirty-year marriage. On that night, we opted for the sound of the ocean lapping at the shore and the sight of slanted moonlight on the cement floor. If only I could have revived the seductress in me and spun a thousand-and-one-nights story to leave him wanting more; if only he could have turned to me and said, "My beloved, you are the only one for me."

But now it's a week later after five days in Israel. We're sitting on cushions in a circle in a Bedouin man's tent, listening to music that sounds like the recordings used in the Middle Eastern dance classes, when, out of the blue, a thin, well-heeled woman wearing a pink linen pantsuit, a dangling necklace of metal beads, and an exotic jingling bracelet to match, a woman not traveling with our group, steps into the center of the temporary dance floor and moves in the style of the belly dance. To my trained eye, she's only had one dance lesson, if that. Though she's flirtatious enough and the object of much attention, there's no roundness to the undulation of her hips and stomach, no soul to her dance.

It's probably a competitive urge, but I feel moved to join her. David watches me rise to my feet. "Go for it," he says. He claps his hands in time to the music. "Oompah," our tour director Shirley says, clapping her hands, too. "Yes. Oompah!" She's the one who arranged this evening in the Bedouin tent where we've broken bread with these men in scarves and robes, our tour group sitting cross-legged, eating hummus, pita, and skewered lamb with another small tour group from England.

I borrow the scarf hanging around David's neck—the black-and-white scarf usually worn on the heads of desert men with a black cord for keeping. *Goddess in pink, move over.* Twirling the scarf over my head and past my hips, I commandeer a major portion of the space provided for dancing. For a moment, I lose awareness of the woman in the pink pantsuit and everything else, then, suddenly, I see that Omar is swaying with me, his fingers clapping the palm of his left hand, his sinuous torso reminiscent of shifting dunes. I toss the scarf back to David, who's watching with curiosity.

Omar and I circle each other: boy meets girl, boy circles girl, girl weaves the web as her arms snake through the air. Surprisingly, I feel shy as a country girl fresh from milking a cow—something rural in my ancestral memory carrying me to the unwanted condition of bashfulness. But his eyes don't leave my face. They instruct me to stay. To be here. Now. This dance is beginning to feel intimate, as though it shouldn't be watched. But gradually, I raise my eyes to his and meet his gaze, which isn't frightening or boorish but rather direct and unflinching. It's like the back of a fingernail brushing slowly across my cheek.

His unexpected tenderness pulls me in. I stay with his gaze. As we dance, our feet become unnecessary. The beat of the hand drum and the melody on the oud sound like someone making love to the strings. This is not child's play. This is not the awkward teenager with slumped shoulders hiding her new height, being pushed to the center of the living room floor at a family gathering to demonstrate the latest move from her ballet lesson. This is not the one who laughs nervously, then rushes to sit back down on the sofa between the safe shoulders of her brother and sisters.

This is a call to be still, to be calm. There's no room for apology. It's time for fluidity, all parts working together. Our eyes are becoming something besides eyes, something unsolid, more like slow lava rolling over the lip of a volcano. The pounding of the drum inserts itself with a 7/8 beat that mesmerizes in the way only a 7/8 beat can mesmerize. The dancing. The drum. The plucked strings expand the sides of the tent until the night comes in to dance with us, its stars slipping beneath the flaps.

Maybe this is how it was in the Beginning when atoms whirled to spark life into being: the creative magnet exerting its force, the female responding. And for a moment, God isn't up in the sky. He's not sitting on a throne in a faraway heaven. He's here looking into a woman's eyes, assuring her of the glory of being female, the one who brings form to God's ideas.

So many times I've hidden in that place where I can't show myself—an exposed snail so bare and squishable outside its shell. But tonight, this man, who is one sliver of God as I am one sliver of God, speaks silently that there is nothing beyond this moment. Only now. Our fingers don't intertwine. Our hands touch only air. The space between us remains open and yet filled at the same time.

PART THREE: 2000

The noisy, single-engine plane noses through what looks like a barricade of clouds. Bold slashes of blue attempt a takeover of the thick, gauzy skies, but the grayness is winning.

"*Mira*," the pilot says suddenly, excitedly, pointing toward the tip of the right wing. "*Un volcán*." Christine, our group leader who sits in the copilot's seat, translates. All eight members of the Eco-Trek tour group strain forward to catch sight of something in our wildest imaginations we never thought we'd see: massive, roily, dust-filled clouds of darkest gray belching out of the earth's interior; molten magma embellished with lines of fire oozing over the volcano's lip. But then, too quickly, it fades in the distance behind us, and the pilot points the plane's nose downward toward the Maizal Jungle in the Oriente of Ecuador. We sink into a sea of even darker gray clouds, drop into a clearing, skid onto an underwater field of grass, and plow through mud. Christine turns to us, pulls a rubber sack toward her, then opens it to a disheveled assortment of knee-high, black rubber boots.

"Always wear these," she instructs, sorting them into pairs, handing them out.

My foot slips around when I stand up in mine, the size too

big, but who's going to complain when we're about to cross a terrain with endless slithering possibilities.

"Members of the tribe are here to take you to the village," she says. "You should know they were a head-hunting tribe until about thirty years ago, but there's nothing to worry about. I've been coming here for a few years now, and I still have mine." She smiles a big smile. "But remember. They're a proud people. It's an honor for each of you to be here among them. Show your utmost respect. I can bring you here because they trust me."

A head-hunting tribe. Maybe this is a conspiracy to bring in more meat for the growing children. My memory sifts through images from Old West movies—shrunken heads, long black hair dangling from a scalp hanging on a branch on a tree next to a tribal village. Fires. Smoke. Frenzied drums.

"Things have changed," she says, as if overhearing my thoughts. I laugh nervously to myself, wondering if everyone else is taking silent measure of their necks.

"One more thing," Christine adds. "Women, don't look directly into the eyes of the men here as they'll mistake that for an invitation to take you into the jungle for big passion."

Big passion. We look at each other with arched eyebrows and mock expressions of disbelief. *I'm a single woman now—no David, no boyfriend. Big passion should sound inviting, but not on the floor of the jungle. I'll keep my eyes to myself.*

When we climb down the airplane stairs to greet three men who are approximately two-thirds my size, they crowd around us—thin, small-boned, waving their hands, shouting in a language I can't understand as I'm contemplating the tropical foliage that seems to be creeping toward the airstrip as we speak. *Tarzan. Swinging vines. Snakes wrapped around tree branches and possibly my neck.* Nevertheless, we follow them at a quick clip on grass-covered paths, across a line of cutter ants, into dugout canoes, across two swollen rivers, back onto paths stamped out of tall grasses, until we reach a clearing with a compound—a lodge built of thin branches with a precisely woven palm-leaf roof. The men show us to our rooms with cement floors, well-brushed corners, and the smell of fumigants keeping insects at bay.

After the breakup of both my first marriage and the rebound romance that followed, I'd made efforts to get on track again physically, emotionally, and mentally. But vestiges of sadness still clung to me. My friend Joy, owner of the metaphysical gift and book store where I worked, knew my state of mind and invited me to join her and some other Park City women on a trip to Peru to visit a shaman. She'd also invited me to join her and her husband, Myles, afterward in Ecuador with another group called Eco-Trek. The Maizal Jungle is the last leg of our six-week journey where we've not only visited Indigenous communities of the Andes and received teachings from keepers of a five-thousand-year-old wisdom, but have participated in numerous healing ceremonies. The healing I received the day before this one—the ritual conducted by Alberto Taxo, a shaman in Quila-jalo—is alive in me still. Some stuck, unyielding place in myself, some dam, some useless fortress wall, has crumbled. And so, that afternoon after we settle into our rooms, when four of us hike on a well-worn path through the jungle that feels like a sauna and arrive at a clear, shallow, broad river, I can't help myself.

"Are there any piranha here?" I ask Christine on an impulse.

"No," she says, eyeing me suspiciously. "Why do you want to know?"

Usually cooperative but feeling impulsive today, I flop back into the clear water to let the slow current carry me. I've always felt at home in this element after taking Red Cross swimming lessons in Lake Mead as a child. I want to be re-baptized, to immerse myself from head to toe, to be cleansed by water and celebrate the way I've been feeling since my healing from Alberto. Something has definitely changed.

Through the drops of splashing water, however, Christine

looks at me with ill-masked horror on her face. Right away, she dives in beside me. Suddenly, remembering she's responsible for any breaking of the code of this jungle and that maybe I've done just that, I think of stopping time and reversing the action. But we're both in the flow of water, which seems harmless enough at the moment, so I relax and give myself over to the current. We float next to each other, the sound of running water in our ears, until we arrive at a widening of the river, the sandy bank, and the shores of the compound. After searching the bottom of the river with one foot to find a secure place to stand, I shake the water off and push wet hair out of my eyes while Christine does the same. She's kind enough not to berate me in front of the two Shuar children looking at us curiously from where they stand at the edge of the river. *Anything could have happened,* her effort at silence says. *You need to respect where we are.* I cringe at the thought of breaking some kind of jungle etiquette (though I pay my dues a week later when I'm flying back to the States and find I've contracted the dreaded giardia, which takes two weeks and a vile antidote to cure).

On our first night in the jungle, my first gaffe behind me, we're treated to a traditional dinner at roughhewn picnic tables set on a cement slab. After dinner, more community members join our dinner staff to demonstrate the old ways of the Shuar people. Christine explains that some of these ways are continued today, though mainly by those wishing to preserve tradition. Dressed in wraparound cloth rather than the bare-breasted jungle wear often seen in *National Geographic*, the native people portray how they used to visit their friends' homes: the way they'd greeted each other with spears, complex choreography, and chanting, and how they'd entertained each other with a brew called chicha made by the Shuar women from manioc root and saliva, which they spat into the mixture and allowed to ferment. "Chicha was carried with them whenever they went for a visit," Christine explains. "And it still is."

Before we're sufficiently prepared to find a gracious way to decline, two of the women approach our table with a half coconut shell of this sour delicacy. *Saliva. Fermented saliva. Save me, somebody.* They seem to be fully expecting our pleasure at being able to share a drop of their strange brew. All thoughts of travel sickness ignored, the members of our tour group pass the shell around and each partake of tradition with a straight face and subtly pinched nostrils.

After the chicha, gratefully, there are two musicians with a guitar and a reed flute who play music from the Andes (the jungle being an extension of the Andes, Christine explains). Several of the Shuar men ask the women in our group to dance. When a rather minuscule older gentleman, with bones more appropriate for a bird, asks me, I remember the caution about eye contact. In the light of four inadequate floodlights shining from each corner of the dance floor, I concentrate on his feet while moving my own and spend much of our dance together laughing internally about how this protective measure defeats the purpose of dancing and getting to know your partner. When he asks me to dance a second time, I can't deal with counting his toes anymore. Impulsively, I reach across to him with my palm up and gesture to him to clap it. It's a game I used to play with my children: 4/4 rhythm, clap your knees, clap your own hands, then trade claps with your partner. At first, he's confused, but after a few more demonstrations, he finally claps my hand back. Then the other. Both of us end up laughing and even hopping around in a circle as if we are children until the music ends. *Except, maybe I'm breaking a taboo here or at least being a disrespectful tourist by playing loose with the native people. I don't know the rules here, except I didn't look into his eyes.*

When the party has been cleared away and the Shuar people disappear, Christine stops me with an amused expression on her face. "Do you know who you were dancing with?"

"No," I say, raising my eyebrows, expressing my innocence.

"That was Whonk. He's the most powerful shaman in the Shuar tribe."

"Oh," I say, suddenly panicked. "Really?"

"Really." She smiles and turns to go to bed, leaving me there to stew in my mental juices. *The most powerful shaman? Good grief. Maybe I did something irreparably wrong by touching the hands of the shaman. If only I'd known who he was before the dance. Maybe I'd have been more careful. But maybe, intimidated by his title, position, and power, I'd have done something unnatural, like kowtowing or bowing or, worse yet, avoiding him. What did it mean to be a shaman here in the jungle? Was he sacred? Untouchable?*

As I pull down the sheets of my bed and search for insect invaders with my flashlight, I think about the word *sacred*. What does that mean? Respect? Awe? Veneration inspired by authority? Sacred has always felt like something external—a higher being out there somewhere, a holier place than the one where I'm standing, or an intermediary between myself and God. It's good to be in South America with these shamans. Good to drink chicha even if it is fermented saliva. It's good to dance with the most powerful shaman. It's also good I hadn't known Whonk's title. There's protocol to worry about. But important as respect is, I always seem more concerned with the sacred code of the Other. There are things that matter to my integrity, like making meaningful contact with strangers.

The next morning, I see Whonk speaking to our translator. In the daylight, I see him with greater clarity. He seems less old, more agile, his skin more honeyed-chestnut brown. There is strength in this man with small bones for his frame, a vitality I hadn't been able to discern in the dim light on the dance floor. He's no longer a tiny man, delicate as a bird, but powerful in his serenity, with his chi, with his at-homeness in the world.

"Please tell him he's a good dancer." I speak up, emboldened by the beauty of the day. "I enjoyed dancing with him but tell him I apologize if I seemed disrespectful."

The translator laughs a belly laugh at what seems to be a mammoth joke. "He was just telling me what a good dancer you are."

I look at Whonk, even at his eyes that wrinkle into a smile on his sun-worn face, two missing teeth evident. I smile my orthodontically corrected, American materialist smile, but at this point, I'm okay with the way my culture has mandated straight teeth. I'm okay with my place in the cosmic order. He and I clap our hands together one last time and laugh, as that's the language we speak together. I sense this is my final and most important healing from the shamans: to have connected to a holy man, not as an acolyte on bended knee in the presence of a sacred totem, but human to human, heart to heart.

When I attend Whonk's ayahuasca ceremony that night, I decide for the first time during my six-week trip of visiting shamans and learning of their ways, not to participate directly in another ceremony. I'm not an ayahuasca tourist—that's not my intention. Nor am I a woman trying to right herself with the world anymore. I'm part of this sacred world. My world is sacred as Whonk's is sacred. My love of dancing is sacred, too.

In the flickering candlelight in the dark of the Maizal Jungle, an understanding comes. No one has the corner on sacred or holy. The whole earth is a holy place—its people, animals, plant life, and geography. It's best to respond to this with gentleness and charity, but we are the ones who know best how to walk through the days and nights of our time here on earth.

The Art of Falling

The rocks didn't look slippery. Wet, a little moss here and there, but not slippery. Usually confident on my rock-hopping feet (though that could be a lie), I skipped, walked, and jumped ever so carefully onto the mainly flat-topped rocks at the edge of the mountain stream—high in the Uintas of Utah, far away from the dry desert. Of course, when I slipped and my foot kicked into the air with the other one not far behind, I didn't think I would end up upside down on my nose against rocks in the stream, blood gushing everywhere. This couldn't be me. I was a fairy princess with gauzy wings flitting and skipping over water and rocks, defying gravity. A dragonfly even, darting and whirling with my helicopter wings. A thing of utmost weightlessness.

So rude to be suddenly crashed into a granite boulder, my delicate nose cracking and snapping and reminding me of the last time I'd tripped over a box in the middle of the night and landed, yet another time, on my delicate nose that has contributed to my vanity through the years. Grass. Long stream grass in front of my eyes. The playfulness of water against the rocks.

Other boulders at eye level. A high scream that I couldn't quite hear as it had to be off in the distance somewhere.

I hadn't fallen. Not me. I was still walking along the side of a tumbling stream, poking my toes here and there, checking for a stray toad or a minnow. This was a movie in slow motion, an actress who looked and felt like me turning upside down just like that from up to down, from tall to short, from airborne to grounded, from the light of day to the red, black, and smeared colors in front of a pair of eyes, the feel of something having been rearranged without that something's permission. This was not my blood on the rock. This was not me on the ground. This was not me being helped up by a man named Bill who resembled my second husband. This was not me leaning against his shoulder, trying to wipe the liquid from my face, the mixture of blood and maybe tears, though these wouldn't be my tears. This was someone else, not me, the graceful fairy princess.

The indignity of falling is beneath the province of a fairy princess. Or that of a dragonfly or a butterfly, one of those fluttery things that have no problem colliding with Mother Earth.

Falling. I'd like to think I don't do it. I like to think I am sure-footed like a gazelle (why do human beings think they can leap like an animal anyway?) and graceful as the most aerodynamically tuned ballerina or squirrel-cape jumper. I like to think of myself as petite and oh so delicate, even though I'm five foot nine and have a wide pelvis and long bones. Truth is, when you're tall, you fall pretty hard. It's a long way to the ground, so covet height not, you people who call yourselves short.

One time in college, I rode on the back of a rented motorcycle with another freshman who didn't have much of a clue about riding motorcycles except to get on it, gas it, and go. We were, however, having a grand ride through the streets of the college town, no helmets, no knee pads, no protective clothing. Those were the days! Face and caution open to the wind! Me holding tightly to the back of his shirt, feeling the rush of the pavement beneath our two wheels, the blur of the shops and cars at the sides of the road.

When he came to an intersection where a railroad track had been almost covered over by asphalt, but not quite, and where small channels had been dug into both sides of each rail to keep trains on the track, he unwittingly turned the motorcycle wheel into the channel rather than driving straight across. The wheel caught. The motorcycle tipped. I flew through the air, as if in suspended animation, being released from gravity, up, up, and up and thinking, "I'm flying. Like a bird. La-ti-dah. What a feeling." Time stopped. Me, my spirit, and my body were enjoying this rare moment in the air. "What a beautiful autumn day. The sun so bright against blue. I'm a leaf fluttering in the air, a thin, wavering, shimmering leaf being gentled to the ground by the sweet fingers of air, the substance where birds can soar and catch currents."

I don't remember what happened to my friend who drove the motorcycle, sorry to say, though he must have suffered only minor damage because he was right by my side, helping me up from the ground. He brushed the gravel from my sweatshirt and the seat of my pants. A few bits of broken leaves in my hair. He took my bloody hands in his. We laughed, sort of. We shrugged our shoulders. He picked up the motorcycle, undamaged, to return it to the rental shop, me on the back once again as the distance was too great to walk, this time creeping along with much more caution. Then, in his borrowed car, he took me to the college infirmary. I had scraped the first layer of skin from my hands and shins, sprained an elbow, and bunged up a knee badly enough to wear a brace. After returning to the dorm, my roommates offered to help me bathe for a week. My sojourn in the air, up, up, and away from the pull of gravity, had ended, after all. I had returned to the ground, to the insistence of gravity.

Time might not be immutable. It can slow and bend and twist when our methodical, clock-like minds stop ticking away relentlessly in times of emergency and adrenaline-pumping threat. It might be possible for a human being to become a bird, to sprout feathers, even if for a split second, and experience the float of momentary wings carving the air. This could be a gift from the inhabitants of the air, letting us be privy to their lives and their joy in the realm of space. This could be a gift from angels, these former humans with present-day wings. Could the act of falling be a strange sort of gift? A chance to be a bird for a split second before gravity has its say? This chance to be an angel (if your imagination includes angels in its repertoire)? Or is this suspension in time between falling and landing simple denial, not accepting the inevitability of the cold, hard ground waiting to receive you?

Falling away. Falling apart. Falling from grace. Falling from favor. Falling from power. Falling off cliffs. Falling from the ends of the earth. Falling action. Falling out. Falling through cracks. Falling to your knees. Falling all over yourself. And yet, falling in love, as well.

To fall. To fall down. To fall behind. To fall into line. To fall for. To fall on. To fall back. A felled tree that has fallen. Fall fashions. Fall crops. To fall back on old habits. To fall prey to. To fall short.

This is a lot of falling. The word *fall* must have caused many non-English speakers a good deal of consternation and confusion. Even Webster must have struggled to come up with a full accounting of the word. It seems to mean many things to many people.

Consider the act of falling. What does it mean to fall? "To drop or come down freely under the influence of gravity," the dictionary says. "To drop oneself to a lower or less erect position." But the word *fall* seems to have more impact or significance than the word *drop*. Many more associations, profound and inane.

Falling can be a momentary or temporary condition as in

falling down and picking yourself up. It can be a permanent or fatal condition such as falling in battle. Falling can mean a small failure, such as in not being able to stand up straight and keep one's self erect, or it can mean Big Failure—someone falling away from the province of grace, never to return to the sublime heights with God, such as in the infamous Adam and Eve in the Garden of Eden. Falling is thus a big word. It means so many things.

What about falling in love? Does that mean that someone has lost their fine sense of balance, dropped to a less erect position (sometimes), and thus lost all reason? Falling in love means giving over to something larger than one's self and surrendering to dictates beyond reason. In that case, falling could be a good thing with benefits. Falling may not always be harsh, or cruel, or awkward, or disgraceful. This word *falling* is a tricky word with many labyrinths and many false stops and starts. Maybe it is a simple matter of falling down and picking yourself up. Maybe it isn't meant to have such profound possibilities as falling from grace, of falling into a black hole, falling through the cracks, never to return.

But falling seems to be part of each of our lives, clumsy or not. We keep falling apart, away, and down. Falling down, and even falling from grace, or do I really fall from grace and whose grace would I be falling from anyway if the Divine is supposed to be loving all of us equally? I don't fall down every day, but it happens often enough for me to think that gravity has too much power over me. That I'm too connected to this earth and to the ideas about falling: that falling is a klutzy, awkward, cumbersome thing to do and only bulls in china shops crash around in this way. It's embarrassing to tell someone that I've fallen again, that I tripped over a box at the post office a few weeks ago, bruised my shin and cut my hands, and had to have my pinky finger x-rayed to see if it was broken. No, it wasn't broken, but it still hurts and doesn't feel like the pinky finger I had before the fall. (Before the fall—those resonant words that have echoed throughout history.) And it all happened so quickly that I didn't even have time to fly through the air and enjoy the art of flying free from the jaws of gravity.

Before the fall. Before the accidents and the errors. Before the dropping away from the state of perfection to imperfection—the act of standing straight as opposed to turning upside down and landing on your face. Falling happens. Losing balance happens. Turning every which way but up, languishing on the floor, on the rocks, on the floor of the office, thinking, "Here I am again, only this isn't me lying here. I'm a fairy princess. Weightless. This is just an error. A snag in the film. A misprint. This isn't me who falls." But then it sounds as if it's not all right to fall, and maybe it's just fine.

THE PRECARIOUS WALK AWAY
FROM MORMONISM
All the Time with a Stitch in My Side

In April 1995, just before leaving for a month-long trip to Slovenia, I had a brief telephone conversation with Linda King Newell, author of *Mormon Enigma: Emma Hale Smith* and chairperson of the annual pilgrimage retreat for Mormon women for which I'd been asked to speak. She reminded me that the theme for the conference was "Our Stitch in Time" and asked if I had a title for my speech. I jokingly said, "What about 'a stitch in my side?'"

"Why not?" she said in her inimitable and gracious way.

"I'll call you if I come up with something better," I said as I hung up, but knew I'd be in Slovenia where it would be an expensive ordeal to make a long-distance call (pre-Internet and cell phone days). This title would have to find a text.

Three days and much thought later, as I sat on the edge of Lake Bled in Slovenia watching white swans glide through the mist at seven o'clock in the morning, I was struck with a title: "The Precarious Walk Away from Mormonism, All the Time with a Stitch in My Side." I laughed at the sound of the words, at the idea, at the audacity of speaking about a walk away from

Mormonism to a group of Mormon women. But I could talk about my wanderings of the last twelve years, my exit from the ward doors to see what I could see in the big wide world. I could talk about my encounters with other "isms"—Taoism, Buddhism, humanism, existentialism, fundamentalism, Sufism, Southern Baptism where the gospel music made me "you go, girl" happy as the choir rocked down the aisle in their yellow robes with gold thread and white satin hoods and my feet tapped out the time. I could mention my search for a religion that didn't insist upon being "the one and only true church of God" and yet could still capture me as Mormonism had. After all, the Gospel of Jesus Christ was my first love. But then, I'd need to talk about my subsequent doubts about fitting into a larger picture, about having no niche in which to curl and sleep and be cared for. I'd have to own up to the loneliness of such a decision and the fact that there's a stitch in my side.

It could be arrogant to think one's story is so important. In China they call a crazy person "a person with only one story to tell." But maybe my struggle with my religion is the only story I truthfully have to tell. Maybe I'm driving myself and my listeners to distraction with my questioning about stitches.

Then I remembered my reasons for writing from the personal vantage point in the first place. I am a person who likes, who loves, who cherishes my safety. Though some may choose not to listen or to read my writing, no one can quarrel with my experience. They can't take it away. It's mine. People have a right to get angry, however, if I try to speak for them—if I try to witness for them. Julia Kristeva, a French critical theorist, says that writers must be aware of "the indignity of speaking for others. We risk the indignation of excluding those others, whether we side with them or oppose them." With that in mind, I decided to trust my intuition at the edge of Lake Bled and speak of that physical sensation of a stitch in my side.

But what does it mean to have a stitch in one's side? It could be a pain from walking or running too fast or from laughing too hard. However it's caused, the stitch in the side hurt me—like a large needle pulling a thread through an unnameable place. Somewhere in my side.

Of course, my imagination took over. The first images I saw were the traditional ones: a needle and thread pulling at disparate pieces of old pajamas, old coats, old blouses, silk ties. Then my mind crossed over to the fantastic—the large needle of God poking into people's sides and trying to connect them to the whole, trying to pull everyone together. For a moment, God was Janus, the Roman god identified with doors, gates, and all beginnings, the one usually represented as having two opposite faces. In this double-faced picture of God, the One, the female facing one direction, the male facing the other, neither beheld the other's face yet neither was able to leave the other's backside. Mother God was sewing on one side while Father God was digging in the fields on the other side, wearing out his overalls so they had to be mended.

Then there were the needles of responsibility sticking in my side. Do this. Do that. Don't be lazy. An idle mind is the devil's workshop. You can't sit still. You can't be a sloth. So much to do. So much time that mustn't go to waste. The needle in my side. God sewing.

Maybe this stitch in my side is God waking me from my walking slumber to assure me there's a God who'll be there when my seams come undone, who'll sew me back together if necessary. God needling me. Mother/Father. One. I'm not sure whether or not I'm a marionette dangling from threads. Maybe I can't walk anywhere without the hand of God directing me. Threads. How they hold me. How I feel those stitches in my side.

The brief text of my own particular life is that, after years of dedication and every-meeting, every-church-job devotion

to the Church of Jesus Christ of Latter-day Saints, I decided—
through a strange, broken-and-knotted-and-broken-and-knot-
ted-again thread of events including a looming divorce and an
alienation from all that I once thought was "true,"—that it was
necessary and compulsory to find my way to God by myself, that
I couldn't really know God unless I had a direct, unsecondhand,
personal knowledge of the One, the Divine, the All, the Absolute. I needed to take this journey alone, even though I might get
lost. Other hardier, sturdier individuals had died or gone insane
before they were wakened by the Divine. I thought I should look
for God everywhere—in nature, in the grace of a hawk's flight,
in the rising and setting of the sun, in the faces of all the people who passed me, in the myriad expressions of the children
of God, be they rich or poor, brown, black, yellow, or white,
be they devout or rebellious, addicts, or homeless. All of these
were manifestations of God, and I mustn't turn my face from
any creation filled with life. I'd grown suspicious of my innocent,
teenage, Las Vegas Fifth Ward, Las Vegas Stake conception of
God, the one that fit into a few pat testimonial phrases that I'd
repeated over and over to distraction, as if I repeated them often
enough, they'd be true. And I'd grown disillusioned when my
spouse, after a few years of marriage, not only didn't believe as I
did but didn't believe at all. I was brokenhearted about the loss
of my seeming innocence.

I wanted to try again. I wanted to explore the Divine without
the rhetoric of exclusivity. I would run away from home. I would
brave the world myself, even as Don Quixote had done. I would
find God.

As I first walked from west to east, so to speak, from my
birth religion to the exploration of the other, I thought it pos-
sible to walk away from the roots that held and succored me.
But how long can one travel east before it becomes west again?
Maybe my struggle is not such an individual, such a particularly
Mormon one.

Story 1

While in Slovenia, I met Melena in a university in Ljubljana. She was a professor in the pedagogical school, the university being separated into pedagogical and philosophical divisions. Melena was gracious in every way, but there was something automatic about her, as if she had been programmed to be nice, to say all the right words to guests from the United States. She was something like a marionette. It takes one to know one. She reminded me of the stereotypes of communism, the form of government that had ruled Yugoslavia before it had been broken into Slovenia (marked by the individual stamp of Josip Broz Tito, a communist revolutionary, controversial leader and statesman) as late as 1990. Melena had been raised with certain concepts. With a certain language. She'd been molded and shaped by idealistic phrases not unlike the ones I'd known. "This is the idea. This is the way life must be lived."

While many of the younger people in Slovenia didn't wear the mark of the past in the same way she did, she seemed trapped by the language she must have listened to for the thirty-five-plus years of her life. She was slightly stiff, eager to please, graciously abrupt, overly polite, and a product of a culture that has rigid ideas about how one must behave and think. I felt a déja vu in her presence. I knew this woman. I recognized something of myself in her.

But I had to ask: Why does some part of me still accept that the Church of Jesus Christ of Latter-day Saints is the "true" church when that stance has always bothered me? That question is always at my back. Always on my tongue. Always there like a stitch in my side. There is always and forever a part of me who fell in love with the gospel of Jesus Christ before she fell in love with anyone or anything else. People were there to nurture, to guide, to encourage me. I learned to dance, to give speeches, to play the piano by accompanying almost everyone who ever sang or played an instrumental solo in our ward. I have been given much. I have been blessed by my country which I call Mormon. I am a Mormon in my blood and in my bones. One ancestor drove the wagon for Joseph Smith—the original prophet of the Church of Jesus Christ of Latter-day Saints. Another was baptized by Hyrum Smith, Joseph Smith's brother, in Nauvoo, Illinois. These men are in my blood. And yet, in a seeming paradox, my great-grandmother was one of the first suffragettes in Utah. A public speaker. A singer for Brigham City holidays who didn't spend enough time at home. My Danish great-grandmother, a convert straight from the Old Country, brewed beer in her basement, even though brewing was not frowned upon in the 1880s the way it is now. Thank God for the variety of ancestors, not all of whose stories would qualify for a Daughters of Utah Pioneers anthology.

We are shaped by the concepts with which we've been raised. Is it possible to emerge into a different sensibility (the notion of a daisy being another flower besides a daisy), or are we forever shaped, as Melena in Slovenia seemed to be, by the rhetoric of our young lives and idealism? The language we learned as children may not be flexible. It may be deeply entrenched. At our cores, we might always speak a language that's internal to our culture alone and only understood by others like us. We may find it impossible to expand beyond the perimeters of this language to create new possibilities for ourselves and others.

Story 2

Ariel Atzil, our tour guide when my first husband, David, and I were in Israel in 1991, was once an Israeli fighter pilot. He was movie-star handsome, intelligent, and the most intense man I'd ever met. Two of his brothers were killed in the Six-Day War, waged in 1967 when the Straits of Tiran were closed to Israeli shipping by Egypt. Catching the United Arab Republic forces by surprise, Israel crippled the Egyptian, Syrian, and Jordanian militaries and killed over twenty thousand troops while losing fewer than one thousand of its own. Ariel and his family lived in constant fear of sending their children off to school. To bring that point closer to home, on some of our tour group's excursions, we'd seen laughing school children on school outings accompanied by parents carrying semiautomatic weapons. While we were there, the palpable hysteria in Israel felt as if it could combust at any time. In the Old City, young Hasids walked through the Arab Quarter at breakneck speed, carrying Uzis, looking at no one, acting as if they could be contaminated or killed if they slowed their pace.

One afternoon when our tour bus took us to a place where there was a spectacular view of Jerusalem, a Palestinian man tried to pull a money-changing scam on one of the older men in our group. The con man was showing bills, counting them out, and double-ending the bills so they seemed twice their value. Ariel shouted at him in Arabic. The voices got louder. Ariel had a gun in a holster at his side. The men were suddenly nose to nose. The Palestinian man was pulling up his tunic as if to procure a weapon, maybe. Everyone ran for the bus. My husband ran interference, grabbed Ariel by the shoulders, pulled him back to the bus, even as he was still shouting and fingering the gun at his side.

That evening at a quiet social in Ariel's home, I asked him why he stayed in Israel when the tension was so intolerable. He replied that he'd lived in Switzerland for two years but hadn't liked it. The people were closed. Hard to know. It was time to read between the lines. Ariel had a cause in Israel. He had something greater than himself for which to fight. Something to live and die for. Dying for a cause must have seemed greater to him than dying in a nice, safe, possibly boring life. He was consumed and alive with his cause.

How necessary is it to have a cause in one's life, a conflict that engages you, that engages me? Maybe our lives matter more if we care deeply about something. The people in the front lines (excuse the war-like metaphors) are heroines or heroes if you like. But if the people in the front lines accomplish their goal, they may be out of a job, as is the case in Eastern Europe where I was when I first thought of the title for my speech. According to Aleš Debeljak, a Slovenian poet who felt he wrote in the shadow of literary giants who had truly suffered for their cause as he had not:

> In a communist regime, constantly eroding under the radical criticism spear-headed by prominent members of the Slovene Writers' Union, young literati were left with little ideological taboos to debunk, almost no political blacklists to challenge, and virtually no censors peeking over their shoulders. They had to design their own responses to a predicament that currently haunts so many Eastern European writers: "How to address broader moral and social dilemmas of the time when they seem to be better dealt with by anti-totalitarian activists?"

While I have many ancestors who crossed the plains for the gospel of Jesus Christ according to the Latter-day Saints, I acknowledge that the world is not so easily defined for me, not so do or die, not so stark in contrasts. Many of these ancestors have been described as noble, as "Freedom Fighters," not unlike the Slovenian partisans during World War II, many of whom lost their lives defending their country and their ideals. But while many have chosen to stay and stand firm within the structure of Mormonism, to be faithful to the ideals of the early pioneers who pushed their handcarts and rode their wagons across the country, others have taken different stances that bear their individual stamp, their own brand of faithfulness within and without the fold in a less-defined world. That would include me, even if I'm still tangled in Mormon thread.

○

As a writer continually searching for ideas, themes from my religion, in particular, and spiritual themes, in general, continue to present themselves to me. A children's book I wrote titled *Legs: The Story of a Giraffe* was chosen as one of the ten best books in Macmillan's spring 1993 catalog by the Seventh-day Adventists, but it didn't sell well to the larger public when critics claimed the book "too sad." Why should two giraffes die, one in the wilds, one in captivity, even if it is a true story? This is a children's book after all, and children shouldn't be burdened by the difficulties of death.

If critics had believed in an eternal life, I thought, what they perceived as the sadness of the book would not seem so sad. But there it was: my assumption of eternal life. I've heard that particular spiritual theme for years. It's like a lullaby I heard as a child. It floats up out of nowhere and feels like music that whispers to me even though I try to sing other songs.

As I've tried to present stories from my religious culture to a wider audience, to help the culture at large see the beauty, complexity, and engagement rather than the oft-times misperceptions, I wonder if the prospects for carving out a niche in a large frame is unpromising. People's perceptions are often stuck in concrete. And, as I stand with my arms stretched out toward both my old world of Mormonism and the other world of many isms, I wonder if I have a home anymore. I may have lost something in my precarious walk away.

The question arises whether anyone can return to a nostalgic past. Home could be an illusion to which one clings. Maybe I'm deluding myself to think I have a home in this world anyway. We're all travelers and students here, and I'm happiest when I consider myself a traveler without the worry of having to belong, to be popular, to be right, to be safe—most of all without the worry about safety.

Maybe it's best to surrender and be still. To make peace with heaven and earth and be a Siddhartha, ferrying travelers and seekers across the river. To be content with not knowing all the answers. But regrettably I'm not quite ready to sit by the river in bliss. I'm still engaged in the search for the "unbearable lightness of being"—the state of existence unencumbered by the weight of having to have meaning.

Milan Kundera, the exiled Czech novelist and author of *The Unbearable Lightness of Being* (an internationally acclaimed novel published in English in 1984), characterizes the modern writer in the Don Quixote gesture. Is this writer noble or foolish as she ventures out into the world to test her own paradigm?

> What she finds, suddenly, is what the modern man and woman finds—a world that no longer fits her expectations, however learned, from religion, society, family, state, philosophy, science, etc. And worse, she finds a collective world actively or passively subverting her images and models for it. The contemporary writer must question a world that tries to force its dogmatic answer on her. That questioning of everything, from external modes of authority to the very motives of the self . . . must be continuous.

But Richard Jackson, a fine poet and a colleague from Vermont College of Fine Arts who took a group of writing students and advisers like me to Slovenia, asks a question: "What sort of poetry can save nations or people and *not* participate in its own self-made imperialism? What sort of poetry can do this and not attempt to establish itself from a falcon's perspective, from a distant and austere Parnassus, looking down upon the very people it should serve?"

So, by taking a walk away from Mormonism, I can't tout myself as a brave soul or as a more valid authority on the subject because I've asked questions. So-called bravery may be a lot of puffery. I can't negate the place, the roots, the ground from which I sprang. It isn't my wish to establish an imperious throne on which I can sit and toss wisdom pearls to the masses. But I have some need to assert my will, a small thing maybe, and an impetuous, immature thing maybe, but I want to know what the word *freedom* means, freedom of choice, free will. But freedom is a lonely place sometimes. When there are no walls around you to hold you in place, no walls to keep you in your niche, you have nothing to tether you to the earth. You have no cause. Just how far can I walk away from Mormonism until I have walked into something I'm not, until I lose myself, pull out the roots that have given me nurture? This is the other side to so-called freedom.

God plucks at me. Pricks my side. I remember seeing a baptismal font in the Baptistery of the Duomo in Florence. It's not like the fonts found in most of today's churches, those used for the purpose of baptism by sprinkling. It is obviously deep enough and large enough for immersion, and part of me thinks, "Aha, just as my teachers told me in Sunday School. The truth after all." But then my traveling companion tells me that baptism by immersion fell into disuse because of the plagues and the concern about spreading disease, not because of some corruption of the church, as I'd always been led to believe.

Story 3

On the last day in Slovenia, when I'm very late trying to catch a train from Ljubljana, I stand in line until I finally reach the woman at the counter and ask for a ticket to Vienna. She tells me something in Slovene I can't understand. I plead with her. "What are you saying?" She repeats her Slovenian, which can't penetrate the folds of my brain. But then, who should show up like Superman and Superman, but two missionaries for the Church of Jesus Christ of Latter-day Saints, from Utah no less. They take me to the right ticket counter, wait while I buy my ticket, and carry my over-heavy bags to the train. Somehow, in the young girl part of my heart, I was glad that these guardian angels were Mormon.

Melena is still committed to the principles of communism, even though the regime has changed to something other than it was after Tito. She's a good woman. She's principled and believes all people should be treated equally and that materialism is an insatiable monster of sorts. She is shaped by these things much as I've been shaped by the communal character of my religion. But in order for me to grow, in order for me not to be static, I must question. That is the way of my being. I don't do it for any other purpose than to transcend old ways of comprehending on the unrelenting path to the Divine. I am, after all, on the path to God, not to a particular church. I need to be prepared for the face, possibly many faces, of God that I'm unable to see. What we see may surprise all of us. It might dash our expectations.

Wallace Stevens, in his poem "Of Modern Poetry," says the poem must question everything it confronts to discover new values, however tentative: "It has to construct a new stage." At the same time it must fight a simple nostalgia for a simpler past: ". . . the scene was set: it repeated what / Was in the script. / Then the theater was changed / To something else. Its past was a souvenir." This could be true of the never-changing principles of the church in which I was raised.

The language I learned was created by the richness of "Sisters, Brothers, the priesthood, the laying on of hands, spirit, testimony, obedience to the Word of God, the building of the Kingdom." I am shaped by these words. I am who I am because of these words, and yet I need to keep questioning them, if only to find the farther reaches of those words, their possibilities.

Words are not cement. They are fluid. They are alive. They can grow and transcend the old meaning.

If "man is now as God once was," as Joseph Smith once spoke in his King Follett address (a Mormon concept that has caused some theological debate), then all things are capable of growth, change, and transcendence, especially our habitual ways of seeing the world. We need to question the assumptions around us, the language we use, the traditions that may have outworn their usefulness. We should also pay tribute to that which is good, that which has blessed our lives.

Maybe all of us are incapable of walking away from what we've been taught. Granted, that could be part of the truth. But I believe there is a bigger truth that surrounds us at this very moment. Maybe we are, indeed, in God's hands, or we are a cell on the body of God as the Hindus say. The truth is in front of me, to the sides of me, as it is behind me in the nostalgic past.

Maybe I need to revise my thinking about the stitch in my side and consider if it's not from laughter after all. Maybe it's God, Buddha, Krishna, Mohammed, the Omnipotent Father, poking me to say that no one can walk away from the One because we're all part of the One. Maybe I've been in too much of a hurry, going somewhere I already am, panting too much, caught on the horns of a dilemma I've created to keep my forehead scrunched, my brow knitted, occupied with attachment or with the idea of one story alone. Stories are stories and will always be told. They're not, in truth, about an infinite number of topics. They are familiar. They center around birth, death, the effort to love or to circumvent hate, and the condition of living with a dilemma such as a stitch in one's side. Maybe God has a larger sense of humor than I'll ever comprehend. Maybe the stitch in my side is a gentle, though sometimes painful, reminder that we are on our way back to something that transcends this planet, this mortal life, these earthly and querulous ways, these confused times. Walking away. Walking toward. God is everywhere. We can't walk away because we're inside of God. East is West and West is East.

I imagine us as pictures on a punched piece of cardboard, the kind we used to thread yarn through when we were young girls, a needle in hand, learning the feel of the needle, the yarn. The Divine Mother is threading each card, keeping the pieces from falling apart. The yarn is filling in the outlines of these pictures of women holding smaller needles—mending, sewing, maintaining, caring, yes, but probing as well. Needle. Thread. A stitch at a time.

AT THE CANNERY

By myself, I'm driving east on I-70, just out of Denver. I'm looking for silos in this flat landscape that reminds me of the desert. The high plains were not all that different from the desert I knew. Hmmm. I'm listening to jazzmeister Herbie Hancock on his new tribute-to-Joni-Mitchell CD, *River*. *You gotta love that Herbie*, I'm thinking. Tina Turner's singing "Edith and the Kingpin," something about victims of typewriters and how the band sounds like typewriters. I laugh to myself. I'm one of those victims who's emerging out of my cave where I write every day to volunteer at the Aurora Cannery, a division of LDS Welfare Services.

Flat roof. American flag. Silos with catwalks against a gem-blue sky. A network of antennae. Probably for shortwave radio/emergency communication with all of Colorado as well as Salt Lake City. When Tina sings her last word, I turn off the radio, then realize I'm fifteen minutes early. I smile at the irony.

o

A few weeks earlier, I'd called my friend Virginia to tell her I'd be visiting Salt Lake for a few days and could we get together?

She suggested we do something besides lunch, something more like our normal life together when I'd been her neighbor. "I've already signed up for a day at the cannery," she said. "Do you want to come along?"

"That would be good," I said. "Like old times."

She and I arrived at 9:15 rather than 9:00 a.m., however. Addresses in Salt Lake City were usually given in grid terms, but not this one. Finally, we'd sighted the telltale tan bricks of an industrial-looking building in an otherwise residential area. We were definitely tardy campers when we walked inside the glass door of Deseret Soap & Detergent. Still we were laughing, full of spring sunshine and exuberance, friends reunited for a few hours.

An imposing man with the name "Larry" embroidered on his blue jumpsuit greeted us. I suspected he'd been in charge for a lot of years, the way he rolled his eyes at the dilettante volunteers who'd entered his domain without the serious intent to match his. He pointed to a sign: "No jewelry allowed, no watches, no cell phones or purses." He pointed to a row of lockers. "Are you ready?" He tapped his foot.

"Almost." We hurriedly stuffed our purses in the lockers, then pinned the keys to our T-shirts. We followed Larry, who padded down the concrete hall on gummy soles. He opened a heavy door. He ushered us into his sacred temple of soap—a gigantic Star Wars–looking warehouse where gargantuan stainless steel contraptions hummed songs of metal on the move and filled boxes of laundry detergent with powder before sealing the cardboard. Solidified ribbons of newly poured soap rolled past on a conveyor belt before being guillotined into rectangles. Everything moved in concert in this factory of moving parts and mechanical arms.

"You'll be working with shampoo today," Larry said.

He assigned Virginia a job taping cardboard boxes with a super-sized tape machine. He told me to keep an eye on the bottles moving down the line toward the spigot dispensing pink shampoo. Then he stood back with his arms folded across the elastic waistband of his jumpsuit to make sure things ran smoothly. But there was trouble in Soap City. When the dour man—who'd been running the operation solo while waiting for us laggards to arrive—launched into his orientation demonstration, there was a snafu. Shampoo bottles flew through the air and bonked against the shiny concrete floor.

The bouncing bottles reminded me of the Three Stooges. I forced down the corners of a breakout grin. We had a Larry, and I felt like Moe ready to break into shtick by elbowing Virginia and saying, "Hey, Curly." But Larry, trusty manager that he was, stepped up to the spigot and jabbed a big red button, which caused more bottles to jam into each other. More empties flew through the air and skittered across the floor.

"Give me a minute," he said, grim under pressure.

I tried to look elsewhere to give him a little room to solve this problem. The true north magnet for me was the long ribbon of soap being slashed by paper-thin blades into rectangles. Hypnotic rhythm. Smooth, sharp cuts forming bars that disappeared into a bulky machine. I felt like a kid in the Magical Land of Deseret Soap & Detergent when a newly minted bar of soap popped out, newly stamped with a beehive.

That was a few weeks ago, but as I sit in the parking lot of the Aurora Cannery not far from Denver International Airport, listening to the peripheral sound of a jet streaming overhead, I'm remembering when I was a Beehive girl in the Mutual Improvement Association. I was taught about the industry of bees who worked, worked, worked for the community (though no one ever said much about the drones who worked, so to speak, only for the queen bee). The beehive was the logo for both the State of Deseret and the Great State of Utah. Ever since I was twelve years old, it ranked high on my list of favorite symbols. There it was again, imprinted on the broadside of a bar of soap—a reminder that in this church, industry was a sacred thing. "When you're helping, you're happy," we sang when I was a child. Work, work, work—a strong Mormon ethic stamped firmly into my own broadsides. The key to a good life was service to others.

I check my watch. Ten minutes to go. Time is ticking more slowly than usual. I find the button to lower the seat back and try to get comfortable while I wait.

After several stops and starts and mumbling under his breath (no expletives—this was a church-run operation after all), Larry, the old hand in this business, had things under control. The march of the bottles began again. This time, each empty stopped in the correct position for a manually operated fill-up to its perfect, right level. Then each was sent on its way to have its top tightened into end-product shape before Virginia hand-loaded them into boxes and taped them shut with her heavy-duty dispenser.

My job was to keep a supply of empty bottles ready for filling and to replenish the bottle-top bin for the man regulating the flow of pink shampoo. I moved the huge open box of bottles from one spot to another (it wasn't heavy, but my efforts could make a good impression for anyone who might be watching) and unloaded it, ready for the assembly line. The man at the spigot kept an eagle eye out to make sure I came nowhere close to being remiss in my duty.

I synchronized my rhythm with the machines and the process: a dancer in a mechanistic *corps de ballet*. I kept the assembly line supplied before the humorless Spigot Man could catch me being lax again. I felt a surge of pride in my competence but then I heard "Pay attention!" Pride goeth before the fall, and I'd let the supply of bottles come dangerously close to the red line. The Spigot Man would soon be bottle-less. Panic hit when I realized the big cardboard boxes with more supplies were taped shut, the open one empty. I had no knife. Fingernails wouldn't work. *Don't panic. Where's Larry?*

I looked around the concrete warehouse/factory. He was in

the northwest corner directing a forklift operator moving pallets of boxes, supervising the loading of trucks destined for the Bishop's Storehouse. I'd been to that store without cash registers. The place where those in need could obtain cheese, bread, meat, canned tomatoes, feminine hygiene products, and soap, of course. But *Larry? I need you.* Luckily, another employee walked by, saw my dilemma, pulled a box cutter from his pocket, and sliced the sealing tape. He helped me carry the unwieldy box and pour its contents into a bin.

Back in business again.

○

By now, the sun on the driver's side of my car is heating up the window glass even though it's cold outside. Like the desert in winter. I wish I had a towel to tuck into a crack at the top, something like a maiden's handkerchief signaling I need the sun to let up. I'm ready to go inside for the canning *du jour.* I've heard that the Greeley tomatoes are the A-one product from the Aurora Cannery, but it's too early in the season for tomatoes. When I look at my watch, it seems as though time has stopped. I shake it, though that's an old-fashioned, useless thing to do with batteries. I'm still early. I breathe deeply, center myself, ease the tension in my shoulders, slow my overactive thoughts. But they, as usual, keep tramping across the open field of my mind. I can't believe I'm sitting here like a faithful Latter-day Saint, waiting to be a cog in the machine. *Why am I doing this? I still have my questions. I still have my arguments.* But then I remind myself that when I hear anyone speaking unfairly about the whole enterprise, I'm there. The Defender. There was that difficult evening in 2002 when I lived in Park City.

I'd been asked to speak to a group of New York women gathered for a week of skiing and aprés-ski who'd expressed curiosity about Mormonism. Would I please present an after-dinner speech on the culture and a brief overview of the theology?

Having been inactive in the practice of my religion for twenty years, I wondered if I was the best person to speak, but I had, after all, come from nineteenth-century pioneer ancestors converted in Wales, England, Denmark, even Massachusetts and Illinois. Some of these hardy forebears had bumped across plains in Conestoga wagons, some had pushed handcarts and worn out their shoes, but all had found something deeply invigorating about the idea of building the Kingdom of God here on earth— something to which they gave their lives, their all, their everything. As they traveled westward, their passion for God became thickly mixed with the blood that flowed through their veins and then into mine. Scratch my skin and you'd find a Mormon there. I'd tried to disaffiliate myself from the religion, frustrated with its challenges to my wide-ranging intellect and my concern for women's voices being underrepresented. My childhood, my roots, tradition, the music, the community, even the language and concepts of the cosmos, however, inhabited too much of my sensibility for me to think I could make a clean break.

The hostess and owner of this never-ending mansion on a hill overlooking Deer Valley opened her doors while old money spoke softly from every corner. A copy of one of my books had been placed at each place setting, purchased as a favor. I was immediately enamored with the savvy group and their willingness to learn, to listen, to treat the Church of Jesus Christ of Latter-day Saints as a worthy subject. I'd been used to other responses—dismissing Mormons as a quaint/weird anomaly of the Other Wild West; decrying the way they sent out their young, naïve, robotic missionaries dressed in funereal suits with those grim plastic name tags on the lapels; denouncing them as an insidious cult of long-john-wearing crazies with Stepford wives. When I'd "left" the church years before, a well-known poet asked, "How can anyone as smart as you still be a Mormon?" I'd surprised myself with an uncharacteristically sharp response. "Do yourself a favor, and don't ask a dumb question like that." Very few outsiders understood the appeal or complex demands of living a life patterned after Christ's teachings in the Mormon format.

But four guests from Salt Lake City had been included—all of whom I knew. One was a high-profile, prominent woman known for her voluble opinions about Utah culture and the ever-present majority population. She was vocal about the divide between Mormons and "non-Mormons," a constant topic of newspaper editorials.

I'd become accustomed to wariness around the fact of my Mormonism. There were relatively few Mormons in the town where I grew up. Even though our family was as regular as apple pie with one mother, one father, and four kids in a tidy and tiny white-plastered house with red shutters, my World War II veteran father who'd served in the navy instructed us children to keep our religion to ourselves. "Too many people don't understand what it's all about. They have cockeyed ideas about who we are." Thus, we kept a tight lip on the subject of our faith. We knew that our belief in Joseph Smith translating the Book of Mormon from gold plates, in his conversations with the Godhead and angels, in latter-day prophets who kept our religion current with God's desires and whom we were taught to obey as our consciences allowed, was something about which people could raise eyebrows. Of course, there was the ever-present topic of polygamy, which everyone loved to roll their eyes about even though the Manifesto of 1890 had withdrawn official permission for new plural marriage. Both my paternal and maternal great-great-grandfathers had been polygamous.

I assess the smudged winter remnants on my windshield, almost dangerous for visibility. I need to get to a gas station after my shift and get the thing washed. Checking my watch again, I see that only one measly minute has passed. I'm rarely early, so this stretch of unfilled time is disconcerting. In that Park City home, I spoke for thirty minutes on the history, the bare bones of the theology, and about the Mormon desire to build the King-dom of God on earth. I spoke of the United Order experiment in Brigham City when everyone's crops were taken to the Bishop's Storehouse to be distributed to all. My great-great-grandfather, I added, had played an essential role. I spoke of the paradox of a hierarchical, patriarchal church that seemed monolithic to the outside who wasn't informed of the deep regard for free agency. I spoke of the paradox of people who seemed so sure of their the-ology and yet who were also taught to seek individual answers from God and to continually search the scriptures and best books to perfect their knowledge. "Once, in 1945," I told them, "when a church magazine announced, 'When our leaders speak, the thinking has been done,' President George Albert Smith repudiated the statement. 'Even to imply that members of the Church are not to do their own thinking,' he wrote in a letter to Dr. J. Raymond Copy, 'is grossly to misrepresent the true ideal of the Church.'" Joseph Smith, the original prophet, had expressed in his personal writings that "the first and fundamental prin-ciple of our holy religion is 'to be free, to embrace all . . . with-out limitation or without being circumscribed or prohibited by the creeds of superstitious notion of men or by the domination of one another,'" and how this applied to all members, not just men.

The women seemed open-minded. They knew little about the religion but seemed genuinely curious during the question-and-answer period. But then the hostess raised her hand. "Why don't Mormons have dinner parties?" she asked, though too many other questions were flying through the air for me to answer. I was beginning to despair of answering anything. I tried to formulate an answer to her what-I-considered-off-the-wall question when one of the women from Salt Lake City waved her hand impatiently.

I called on her, then realized she'd raised her hand to speak, not to question. "You're not talking about the reality," she stood to say. "You're not talking about the rednecks from the rural part of the state who have no conception of separation of church and state, who take a lion's share of control over the legislature—the ones who vote for guns to be allowed on the university campus and think that by their very numbers they can run things however they see fit. You're not addressing the problems in education and in a fair representation of the opposing point of view."

"I wasn't asked to address the problems," I said, trying not to be defensive. "I was giving an overview of the culture and the theology. Of course, there are problems, but that's a subject for another lecture."

I hadn't expressed my concern with the Mormon claim of being "the only true church," a stance which made me uneasy as it created an unnecessary divisiveness with other religions, or with the insensitivity that occurred when a few ill-mannered Mormon children in Utah taunted non-Mormon children for being ignorant to "the truth." I knew people who were used to being the majority and used to their own language and conception of right and wrong. And many non-members felt that members of the Church of Jesus Christ of Latter-day Saints were only interested in them as possible converts, not as friends. Back in the seventies, a move to Utah challenged Mormon newcomers as well as non-members. "But please," I wanted to say to that woman, "Utah wasn't the first place in the world having to deal with majority vs. minority. Consider Croatia and Bosnia-Herzegovina, India and Pakistan, North Ireland, even Boston."

The fact that people seemed very sure about who and what Mormons were had become a source of irritation. I myself had played that game. I'd looked down my nose, not being native to the Utah culture, after all. I'd taken a sophisticated stance and sniffed at young couples with overly large families using up the educational resources at the school without paying a fair share of the burden, no tax penalty for large families (Utah having one of the lowest percentages of money spent for education per child in the United States). But while I was living in Park City and gradually, almost subterraneously, reconsidering my roots, I'd also been coming to an awareness that I had an immature understanding of my religion and of Jesus Christ. He not only said, "Feed my sheep" and provided fishes and loaves but was a source of solace and salvation I was only beginning to comprehend.

The hostess raised her hand again. "Please tell us why Mormons don't have dinner parties. I really want to know."

"It's not that they don't have dinner parties," I began, still torn by the challenge from the Salt Lake woman, her words on the cusp of my mind. "Mormons are very social, actually, especially among themselves. Their entertaining, however, is done on a practical level as they're very busy with families and church service." I stalled, trying to stay focused, trying not to short out from the demands of being the authority on a complex subject. "They're busy taking care of the sick, the dying, baking potato casseroles for funeral dinners, working at canneries, going to temples to renew covenants and honor their ancestry by unbinding the knotted links in the genealogy of the world."

My words were going nowhere. "Also, sumptuous dinner parties presuppose a familiarity with fine wines. Some Mormons have no objection to providing wine for their guests while drinking none of it themselves. Some tell their guests to bring what they want to drink, though this makes for an awkward dinner party."

A jungle of hands went up. I felt hunted. I didn't want to stand there anymore. I'd subjected myself to old wounds in my psyche. I'd left this religion.

"I'm sure I've taken more than my time," I finally said, vowing never to accept that kind of invitation again. "Thank you for inviting me tonight and for your interest. Feel free to talk to me afterwards."

o

There's still five minutes before I'm due to sign in at the cannery and stash my belongings. I might as well close my eyes. I could turn on the Herbie Hancock CD again, but I'm not in the mood. I roll down my window a smidge because the magnifying-glass sun's almost burning my shoulder. The cool breeze helps.

A few summers after my speech in Park City, on a hot July day in 2004, I drove through Provo Canyon to Robert Redford's Sundance resort to hear the caustic columnist Molly Ivins speak. I wouldn't want to be on the wrong side of her tongue, though I suspected she wasn't a total sidewinder beneath the lingo. When I arrived at the Tree Room, I saw the woman from Salt Lake who'd been so outspoken at the Park City dinner two years earlier. We exchanged greetings, though her response still burned hot in my memory. She'd seemed dismissive, sure of her position, even arrogant, and I could be good at holding a grudge. I took my assigned seat, gratefully not next to hers.

After a sumptuous brunch where prime rib was sliced onto plates next to a selection of opulent fruits, vegetables, sauces, and puff pastries, the plates were cleared and the crowd quieted to hear a speech from the lively Molly. Touring to promote her latest book, *Who Let the Dogs In?*, she took us on a brief, wild ride to visit the unruly characters in politics, including the top dog known as Dubya. Afterward, she asked for questions. A man raised his hand and asked, "Is Karl Rove an undercover emissary for the Mormon Church in Washington, DC?"

"Hell, no," she said. "He goes to some Presbyterian church, something like that, and doesn't have anything to do with the Mormons. Where'd you get that idea?" The next part of her response was a cause for me to open my mouth in astonishment. "And furthermore," she said, "I think people say things about the Mormons they'd never say about a Jew or a Catholic or whatever they are. There's a lot of disrespect."

Molly Ivins said that? And the Salt Lake City heckler heard it?

Yes. I wanted to raise a triumphant fist. *Yes.*

○

I had no intention of "going back" to my longtime religion when I bought a house in Salt Lake City in December of 2002. I'd lived in the city from 1970 to 1990. This was the place where my first husband and I had raised our three sons before moving to Colorado and going through divorce proceedings. But I'd been living in contrast to those beliefs for almost twenty years. In one of my cross-country moves after my divorce in 1997, I tried Park City to be closer to my younger sister but not too entangled with my religious roots. Then I impulsively married a local man, trying to right the ship. The marriage lasted twenty-one months and was devastatingly disappointing. Not knowing where I belonged, I moved back to Salt Lake to be close to old friends and well-established networks. I needed something when so much else had failed.

But after ten months of hiking and biking and sometimes attending other churches on Sunday mornings, one day I smelled winter coming, thus signaling the end of crisp autumn days. I noticed a change in the light. Sunday mornings had become like other people's Saturday nights. The dawning of the Sabbath had always meant it was time to get ready for church, and I often felt restless in those early hours. A lifetime of habit had made its indelible mark.

On that particular Sunday, a neighbor, another divorced woman, called to invite me to sing in the ward choir with her. "Singing is good for the soul," she said, probably hearing overtones of depression in my voice. On a whim, I decided to go along, possibly influenced by my readings of Carl Jung and the Dalai Lama who both spoke of reclaiming one's roots. After all, I could keep to myself in the choir and not get caught up in the rigmarole of being called to a church position or answering questions as to my worthiness. I did love music and the chance to sing. But after a few weeks, when we were told we'd actually be singing in sacrament meeting, the game plan changed.

Walking into that meeting by myself, walking into that lair of "happy families" sitting shoulder to shoulder on the benches, felt like walking the gauntlet—a self-conscious sinner returning to the chapel with a sign around her neck: "I am alone; I'm not with my family; I'm not like the rest of you anymore."

I walked tall, pretending immunity to this all-too-familiar setting with the organ playing prelude music and people chatting amiably before the meeting. I'd known what it was like to sit in this particular nest with my own family—secure, safe, Mother Hen gathering her polished chicks with shined shoes and combed hair around her, tucking them under her wing, urging them to think about Jesus during the sacrament rather than play with Nintendo or draw giraffes and tigers with crayons.

I walked to the choir seats on the speaker's stand. I didn't look right or left, but took my seat cursorily, basically shy as well as feeling like a displaced person. Facing all of those trimmed and shaved Latter-day Saints where, at first glance, I could detect little obvious diversity, I took a deep breath to keep from weeping in front of everyone. As I fought tears, a man who'd been sitting behind me at the rehearsals walked towards me. He held out his hand. "Hi," he said. "My name's Jim Pearce. I just want to say it's nice to have you here. My wife and I have heard you playing the piano when your windows are open and we've been out walking. We'd love to hear more sometime."

"That's nice," I mumbled, as exposed as a snail without its shell. My protective armor was not in place. There are moments when things change, when there's an opening, a little shaft of light, a recognition, the guard is down and the tide comes in with a wave that curves in a different way than any other wave before it. Jim could have approached me another time and our exchange would have been idle talk. Something about him or the moment and its timing caught me by complete surprise.

"I play the banjo," he added. "Maybe you'll accompany me

sometime." Then it was time for the meeting to start. He turned to go back to his seat in the tenor section.

After he sat down, the congregation sang the opening song. "Love at Home." I averted my face, tried to stay the tears, though they were coming fast. This was a song I'd sung many times. This chapel was my home, my childhood, my family. I surveyed the people when I dared through the wet veil over my eyes, not quite able to focus, but somehow seeing something more than the concrete wall of self-righteousness I experienced when I first walked in. Those were individuals out there, not just a brick wall of conformity. It wasn't fair to lump them into one monolithic unit designed to make me feel uncomfortable because I'd strayed from the path.

A few days later, when Jim's wife, Virginia, called to ask if they could come by for a visit, I didn't quite know what to do with myself. After the meeting where the choir had sung, Belle, my neighbor, told me that Jim's wife was the daughter of President Gordon B. Hinckley, the current president of the Church of Jesus Christ of Latter-day Saints. I felt briefly like the duck girl from the village who had been noticed by the daughter of the king. I'd grown up bearing my testimony of the Gospel every first Sunday of the month, saying how I was grateful for a prophet to lead the church. As cynical as I was, I could still be impressed, even touched, by the thought of having the daughter of the prophet grace the threshold of my home.

During the following few years of living alone in Salt Lake City, Jim and Virginia were like two patient photographers waiting for a wounded animal to come out of its lair. They never prodded me with a stick. They helped me feel safe by saving a seat next to them on Sundays. I felt as if I could be myself and that I wouldn't be forced into anything. "We're not here to change you," Virginia said. "We like who you are."

Also during those years, Virginia, another friend named Laurel Olsen, and I had volunteered several times together at

Welfare Square, one of the church-related services I could render with no hesitation. We'd bagged bread in the bakery, catching slices after they passed through rows of sharp blades and easing them into a plastic bag. We'd helped package fruit drink powder on a day when another machine was acting up and granules of cherry-colored powder sprayed onto the floor, under our feet, so that when we walked we crunched. We'd toured the cheese factory and were told about Atmit, an indigenous Ethiopian porridge of oats, honey, and milk, reformulated by the Deseret Dairy from oat flour, powdered milk, sugar, salt, vitamins, and minerals. Six hundred tons had been shipped to Ethiopia in 2003 to aid children whose digestive systems had almost completely shut down. Given two tablespoons every two hours about eight times a day by a team of doctors, nurses, and other volunteers, the children graduated to something more substantial. Atmit had also been sent to Uganda, Israel, Sudan, Niger, Southeast Asia, Bangladesh, Chad, and the Gaza Strip.

○

It's time for my shift at the wet pack cannery. Finally. I raise the back of the seat, grab my purse, and climb out of the car. A few strangers are gathered at the front doors. Not in the mood to socialize just yet, I lean back against the cold metal of my car and fold my arms across my jacket. I'm living in Denver now, close to my three sons—the Wild Barber Bunch—their wives, four grandchildren, and my first husband, David, who is, now that the battle cries have faded, a good friend. I'm trying to work out what it means to be a family again when Mother and Father aren't married anymore. I love my sons too much to be away from them. It's satisfying to feel as if we're united again. I'm still going to church, though I sometimes feel peripheral, as if I were supposed to be at the center of something and am not. But people can feel lonely, and isn't it the higher purpose to reach out and be a friend rather than wait for one to show up at your door?

The cold from the metal is seeping through my jeans, making my legs feel like ice, a wake-up call to go inside and practice welfare—something that benefits both the giver and the receiver. I'm happy to be here, even though I still feel a stranger, an imposter, in this role. But as I'm walking toward the glass doors, I think of how, just a week ago, I'd taken the bus to my office. That morning it seemed as though all of Africa was aboard, no one speaking a word of English, the aisles jammed with strollers, women with babes in their arms, tall, thin men. About five stops down the line in front of the New Covenant Church (which served the Ethiopian Orthodox Church community—people dressed in white ceremonial robes sometimes lingered outside the building on certain Sunday mornings), everyone disembarked—the women juggling their babies and barking orders to the willowy men. When they'd cleared the exits, a somewhat bedraggled white man boarded and sat behind me. I surmised he was en route to the VA Hospital not much further along the line, that he was probably a Viet Nam vet. I'd met so many of them on the Number 10 bus line. "Must be some kind of church meeting," I said, expressing my curiosity out loud, "but then, it's a Friday morning."

"No," he answered. "They've probably come for food."

I'd gazed after the last of the people streaming across the street and entering the church. *Feed my children. Feed my sheep. The loaves and the fishes. Give them this day their daily bread. Feed them. Take care of their hunger, and you will be filled with Spirit.*

Spirit shows its face in the most unlikely places and times. I first became acquainted with it as a child when I prayed to God, my Father and Friend. I trusted He would catch me if I fell, that He cared about my well-being, that each creature was of His making and therefore beloved by Him. Beneficence reigned beyond the staging of this world.

I'd also heard my father, who served as bishop of the Boulder

City Ward, which met in an old wooden church building small enough to be transported on wheels from the town of Henderson, talking about travelers who were stranded. He'd given them money. He'd arranged shelter. I'd accompanied him on Saturday morning as he directed the building of a brick chapel because he was bishop, not because he knew the contracting business. Members of the ward came out to help, some of them knowledgeable about construction, most not. He was a good shepherd to his flock, a man who could be filled with Spirit as he tended to people's needs and their souls. Once, late at night, I overheard him talking to my mother after he'd been gone all evening.

"He shot himself in the head," my father said. "Do you have any idea what it's like to pick up the pieces of someone who's blown off his head?"

"He's lucky to have you, even if he's gone," my mother said.

"I wish I'd known he'd hit bottom," my father said. "I wish he'd at least have called me first."

○

And so it is that I'm moved to spend a day at the Aurora Cannery, one of a network of over 750 storehouses, canneries, thrift stores and family-services providers. I'm the first from my ward to walk through the doors for the morning shift. The manager directs me to a row of black rubber boots hanging upside down on poles and warns me to be careful stepping over the orange and yellow hoses. Unsupervised, I meander through the facility, surveying large stainless steel baskets next to voluminous pressure cookers, cardboard boxes filled with Ball lids, a row of emergency buttons, a stainless steel table top with twenty round hole cutouts at its edge.

The six women assigned to the round table are short, tall, wide, hefty, wiry. They could be doctors or lawyers for all I know, their hair and most of their features hidden inside of their gauzy shower caps. We stuff mounds of ground beef into tin cans, then send them down the line where lids are sealed and pressure cookers steam. We laugh and make smart remarks. We're sisters. Three hours later, we clean the room with pressure hoses and pressurized hot water. There are squeegees to clean the floor, to push the water and remaining bits of ground beef into a drain in the center of the floor. When everything is spic and span and I've retrieved my purse, I take the outside sidewalk to the dry pack wing to check it out.

"Sister Carlson," her standard plastic name tag reads, is seated at a rectangle folding table in a cavernous warehouse. She greets me cheerfully. I ask her a few questions about the operation, and it's like I've turned on a spigot. "Mesa, Arizona," she says with high enthusiasm, "has a huge welfare cannery with a monster truck packed and ready to go at all times. When a tornado, earthquake, or hurricane is being forecast, a truck will be on the road before the storm even touches the ground."

Resting her elbows on the table, she grins with delight: "Two churches were listed by the media as being the main source of help to those hit by Katrina, one of them the Mormon Church, the other the Church of Jesus Christ of Latter-day Saints. They're one and the same!" She laughs a can-you-believe-it laugh. "The genius of this system is that there's someone to receive goods on the other end who knows how to distribute and deliver them where they're needed."

I used to tire of what I considered to be a certain smugness, this Dudley Do-Right infatuation with one's goodness and accomplishments. Today, though, I respect her pride and dedication. Today, I don't feel separate from, above, or below Sister Carlson. Oh, so subtly and gradually, I'm being folded back into the fold. I've given up resistance and my idea of supremacy somewhere along the way.

As I depart for the parking lot, I read a poster in the foyer, something written by a Sister Jean Christensen while serving a Philippine mission. "Ultimately, I sense I have only . . . been whole when I've divided myself among those who needed me. I've only stood tall when I've stooped to help those that needed lifting." There had been a time when I'd have thought, "How saccharine. Give me a break, Mary Poppins," but today I set my cynicism aside. *To be saved spiritually, people need to be saved temporally. Feed my sheep. We are one. Love one another.*

As I drive away from the Aurora Cannery listening to Herbie Hancock's incomparable piano accompany Corinne Bailey Rae, who's now singing the title track "River" (about "coming-on Christmas" and the upset over lost love), that vulnerable part of myself rises, the part that gets kidnapped by duality, like is this the right way to live life or am I only kidding myself with unreal idealism? I scan my emotional interior for that hard edge in myself, the dependable part that'll keep me from going too soft. Maybe jazz will save me. *Turn up the volume. Blow those horns.* "I wish there were a river I could skate away on," Corinne wails. But today I'm immune to the sadness those lines have elicited in the past. Been there, done the blues, and, at this particular moment, don't share that sentiment.

SWEETGRASS

"Could we stop in Mt. Pleasant?" I ask Bill, my second husband, lucky guy. He's steering our car along the edge of the Atlantic Ocean while I watch the eternal flirtation between tide and shore. "What if we check out those baskets?"

"Haven't we seen enough today?"

"But a sweetgrass basket. They're famous." I'd been reading some tourist information, after all. "They're almost identical to coil baskets made by the Wolof people in Senegal."

"What do you know about the Wolof people or Senegal?" he asks in a tone I interpret as tired or even sarcastic. "And, tell me the truth, do you really need a basket?"

Admittedly, I was known for my zealous shopping habits, my penchant to get sucked into a new place and try to take it all home with me. A desk clerk at Kiawah Island had told me about the baskets. "Their long narrow leaf blades called 'treads' are woven into rows of coils," she'd explained, handing me the pamphlet I now held on my lap, "then sewn together with strips of palm leaf. Sometimes the basket makers reinforce the insides with black rush."

"So?" Bill is waiting for an answer.

"No one needs more than they have, I understand. You've said that. But . . ."

I'm quiet for a while. There's nothing more to do than sit on the passenger side of the car, folding and unfolding the pamphlet. But when the brochure lies open on my lap, accessible to my eyes, I can't help but read on. "The enslaved Africans in this area were credited for the success of the American Rice Kingdom. They turned rice into the main cash crop of South Carolina. They used fanner baskets to toss rice into the air, thus separating grains from chaff—an art form learned in the West African Rice Kingdoms—Senegal to the Ivory Coast to the mouth of the Congo River. They were called Gullah and Geechees in South Carolina, brought here to work the fertile coastal area. Both men and women were more valuable as slaves if they knew how to pull stitches tight and firm to make strong baskets."

Granted, I'm avoiding the topic of our crumbling, about-to-end marriage of two years.

In a last-ditch effort at honoring the state of matrimony, Bill and I had planned a trip to Charleston. What could be better than gracious architecture, rich history, and Southern hospitality, though nobody was talking about Charleston being eighteenth-century America's largest slave market center. We'd booked a room at Kiawah Island, a fancy resort complex, and are now driving on the old Ocean Highway toward Mt. Pleasant. Some cars and trucks pass us with Confederate flags tied to their bumpers. This is not something I've seen in the West, where we've both lived forever. "We'll show you who won the war," they seem to be saying. This belligerence makes me feel uneasy.

But then we see a sign at the edge of the highway: "Sweetgrass Basket Highway, 35 miles per hour."

I crane my neck to check out a deserted basket stand we are passing—no sign of sweetgrass art hanging from its nails and rickety arms of wood. No wares in sight, probably packed away in trunks of cars or in blue plastic bins in vans parked in an alley. "The basket ladies must have gone to a late lunch."

"We need to get back," Bill says, turning on the blinker for a left-hand turn. "I'm tired of driving."

"These people knew rice," I tell him and want to make a little song with those words, sing it to him to enchant him into looking at sweetgrass baskets when we find an open stand. But he's already decided my little songs are weird. I've already decided he doesn't understand my need for little songs.

"Africa inhabited this territory," I continue to read out loud. "More and more slaves were brought to insure the success of rice. Sea island people took charge when plantation owners, afraid of yellow fever and malaria bred in the low-lying swamps, returned to Charleston."

My romantic sense of triumph over adversity tells me that they "hightailed it back to Charleston." *Sea island people.* That phrase could morph into something.

"Maybe . . ." I'm carefully disguising a last-chance plea to change his mind. "Can we find just one stand that's open?"

Beneath the bill of his baseball cap, he keeps his eyes on the road.

I feel the need for a basket blessed by sweetness, something like the smell of the ocean when the breeze is stiff, the smell of morning before the sun rises and the dampness from high tide evaporates. Sweet sounds good. Sweetgrass. We drive past the dunes and lapping waves of the Atlantic, the windows open, the salty aroma of sea wind filling the rented car, almost erasing the scent of chemically sprayed air freshener, former occupants and difficulties.

○

We stop for an early dinner. Bill wants softshell crab. Tis the season, after all. We are seated at a small square table in a run-of-the-mill roadside place with a run-of-the-mill crowd of tourists.

I notice a group of thirteen or fourteen Black women sitting at a long table. It isn't hard to overhear their excited talk.

I try not to eavesdrop but the sound of their rich voices pulls on me, musician-in-every-pore that I am, lover of any and every thing with a good melody and an interesting beat. These women are of all sizes, some of them filling more than their chairs, a few ample bosoms resting on the edge of the table. In the midst of cotton plaid, stripes, yellow housedresses, and a few pant-suits, the women's voices drift like snatches of melody across the room, something about singing in a competition.

Unable to concentrate on the menu, I rise as if in a trance and walk toward their table, Bill calling after me, "Where are you going now?" I almost float to the long table where the ladies' voices are like the Pied Piper sending out a call. I can't help myself.

As I approach the table, the conversation runs thick. After I stand there for a minute, mesmerized, no intention of going away anytime soon, a thin woman dressed in a light tan jacket, her graying hair framing her time-worn face, looks up and smiles a pleasant smile. The woman to her side has an open mouth, holding the next word, maybe stunned that her conversation has been interrupted by a stranger, especially one standing there waiting as if it were her right to do so.

"Excuse me," I begin. The rest of the ladies stop talking to peer over their water glasses and look down at our end of the table. "I couldn't help but hear you talking about choirs. Are you ladies in a choir?"

"Are we in a choir?" the woman in tan echoes my question. "Does a dog bark?"

"Right on, sister," a few voices chime in. Everyone laughs. Mutual agreement. A chorus of pleasure. The tension has been broken.

"We're the best." The woman seated on the corner next to me speaks up. "We're going to show those Georgia people. Battle of the Choirs, and we'll rise victorious." She laughs out loud. I can imagine the crown of victory on her head, glittering gold.

"Is it possible to hear you sing? Maybe rehearsing?" I ask with great hopes, even while suspecting I could be seen as bossy, thinking they need to stop everything and pay attention to my questions. "I love gospel choirs. You are a gospel choir, I'm guessing?"

"That's right, honey. We're making a trip over to Georgia in two days for the spring competition. Gone like a bird. Won't be around for you to hear us. Sorry."

"I wish you luck," I say, wanting to join up and go to Georgia. But just then, "The Devil Went Down to Georgia" flits through my mind, the Charlie Daniels fiddle version. I have no business intruding upon these women. No invitation had been issued. But I still would love to be a speck on a shoulder at their competition or a driver on their bus carrying them to their destination—that is, if they are going on a bus. There are too many for a minivan.

Nonetheless, I'm an outsider here. I thank them for their time and wish them victory, and, as I walk back to our table, Rosa Parks is on my mind, sitting on the front seat of a bus, sitting beneath signs that read, "We reserve the right to refuse service . . ."—that historical wall of segregation that anyone over fifty has heard about. I'd read about Rosa Parks and Emmett Till. I'd heard the sermon about having a dream.

Thank goodness for music. It's something made for everybody. These women have aligned themselves with a music born from suffering and persecution. But I'm drawn to it, too. We all love music, no matter who created it. There must be a place in which all people can stand together, where nothing separates us, no barriers.

○

A storyteller named Mary Ritchie once said that sweetgrass is the hair of our Mother: each strand alone not as strong as when it's braided with other strands. Sweetgrass has a vanilla fragrance. It grows wild in wet meadows and at the edges of sloughs and marshes and bogs, on shaded streambanks and lakeshores in Europe, Asia, and North America. It also grows in bands not far from the high tide line, usually out of sight of the vast ocean and behind the first dune. It flourishes in company rather than solitude.

Holy grass. Mary's grass. Vanilla grass. Manna grass. Bison grass. Sweet, sweet aroma that's pungent after harvesting, even more pungent when dried and moistened. It's pleasing, this sweetgrass. When it's burned, prayers, thoughts, and wishes rise with the smoke, spiral into the air in a translucent column of white, and ascend to the Creator who will listen when the sweetgrass speaks.

Native American medicine men kept it in their pouches with roots and herbs, sweetgrass being one in a group of four healing plants along with tobacco, cedar, and sage.

Believed to have great power, it was often woven into ceremonial baskets. Sweetgrass kept the basket strong. In those times, when a grass gatherer pulled the grass out of its roots, like knives from their sheaths, she understood its power and made a tobacco offering to give something back in exchange.

o

It's now Sunday morning, and we're driving around Port Royal. Bill is helping me look for a church. A place where local Black communities worship, specifically descendants of the Gullah people. Since I've heard about them a few months before, not quite sure where I've heard about them, I want to be with Gullahs. Admittedly, my soul believes there is some straight-to-God purity to be found.

My soul also longs for a tabula rasa between me and Bill—a clean slate, a new beginning—but that only happens with the first breath after leaving a mother's womb. He and I've chosen not to see how we're the same. The main thing we see is our differences. We're committed to maintaining them: I like green, he likes blue. Whatever comparisons we can make. This twenty-month marriage has been coming apart stitch by stitch. Too much baggage, too much prehistory. It seems a withering thing, dying from lack of nourishment, becoming a "you and me" thing rather than an "us" thing.

In the last few days, we've been staying in the confines of our plush room, complete with acres and acres of golf course, sand dunes, gigantic sprawling oaks and palm trees. The sadness has been creeping back, slowly inching up on me. The earth had abandoned my feet when my first marriage of thirty-three years ended. I was unmoored. Space walking. Not finding a place for my feet or believing in a receiving place for my heart, even when I married Bill. I'm not made for the end of relationships.

I feel isolated and odd. I'm around-the-bend about music, and I'm looking for Gullah people. That's a fool's errand, and they're not a tourist stop. I'm dissimilar from them: roots, songs, a different sense of being in the world, and contrasting skin color. Bill and I aren't the same either. He's Jewish, and I was raised Mormon, two disparate cultures though Mormons feel a kinship with Jews—their own Dead Sea, their Zion, their own Gentiles. Even if I have a great-grandmother who wrapped a menorah in a blanket in her wooden steamer trunk when migrating to Utah from Denmark in the 1800s, a line has been drawn between us— cultural differences, my way, your way. But even Black people compare themselves to each other—high yellow, chocolate, caramel, olive brown, ebony, coal black. Colorism.

I've also heard things said and implied: My dad's worth more than your dad. My skin's better than yours. My God is the only God, and you are thus an infidel.

We're all made of the same chemistry even though we're all different. Your nose is longer than mine; there's thinner or thicker hair on your head, ad infinitum. Somewhere, buried in the human psyche, there seems to be a tendency to make comparisons—purer, closer to holiness, more valuable—and to rate what is superior or inferior. There must be a way to transcend this insanity of pointing fingers, calling names, partitioning, comparing, and ridiculing because of differences.

But I digress. Back to our search for a small church in Port Royal. As we'd flown into Charleston, in a break between covert tears, which I tried to hide while reading the pages of an in-flight magazine, I told Bill the two things I most wanted to do on our trip: (1) go to a good blues club in Charleston; (2) find a small, out-of-the-way African American church where I could find descendants of the Gullah people—the ones whom I'd read had dreams about catching the moon with a fish net, the people who could convince flowers to sing and trees to fly, the men who could carve birds that lifted out of their hands and flapped their wings up and away.

Number two is what we're doing this morning—driving up and down wide, gravelly, uncurbed roads in Port Royal, the place where Union troops established a base in November of 1861 and where many escaped slaves known as "contrabands," joined the Union Army as laborers, cooks, teamsters, and servants. From a long-ago history book, I remember President Lincoln had opposed the idea of Black people being accepted into the army, fearing this move would push border states like Missouri over to the Confederacy. Some said a Black man couldn't be trained to fight as well as a white soldier, even though Frederick Douglass, the abolitionist leader escaped from slavery, had said, "We are ready and would go."

So much history on these wide, looping roads on a Sunday morning where so much still seems to be asleep, so many feet trampling over this ground before we ever arrived. Major General David Hunter took command of Port Royal in March 1862. Short on regular troops, he recruited contrabands into a segregated combat unit. President Lincoln, standing by his decision, wouldn't authorize funding to pay these troops. In January 1863, however, he made a dramatic shift in policy with the Emancipation Proclamation, liberating enslaved people in those areas still in rebellion and saying that all free men "will be received into the armed services of the United States." The Black regiment celebrated by singing "My country 'tis of thee, sweet land of liberty" on this, the first day of freedom, some for the first time. Sweetgrass. Sweet liberty. When the war ended, however, the "sweet land of liberty" closed its doors again. In and out. Up and down.

And here we are in that same place, me feeling my passion for a celebration of life and pleading to higher power for the world to be a better place. I want to experience worship different from what I've known in my Latter-day Saint childhood, which, while imbedded with spirit and a certain gentleness, sometimes seems pale and formulaic. I feel the urge to shout "Hallelujah" and feel the music rise up from my toes. I want to tell the people in one of these Black churches in South Carolina that I'm sorry for the arrogance, impudence, rudeness, cruelty, and hatred on the basis of skin color.

I must pause, though. I have no claim to be assigned the role of Crusader. I've struggled with a racist inside of me. I'm not immune to thinking my white skin makes me superior, even though no one overtly taught me to think that way. I'm ashamed of the time in high school in 1957 when I told my English teacher—a man raised in the South—that I needed to be allowed to move away from the Black girl sitting next to me in class because she hadn't had a bath in a long time. He'd shaken his head vigorously in the affirmative, much more than casually. "I understand," he said. We became partners in righteous calumny, in our mutual act of settling the reputation of someone darker than ourselves, no mention of individual personal hygiene. He assigned me a new seat.

Later, and I wish there'd never been that time at a Las Vegas high school play's cast party in 1959, I accepted a dance with a genteel Black boy who'd helped with the play's staging. But I didn't have the confidence to back up my high-flying ideals that all are equal under the sun. I didn't have confidence, period, at that point in time, viewing my physical self as an awkward amphibian. I lived at the margins of popularity already and didn't want to do anything to call further attention to that fact. But still, I'd said yes when the boy asked me to dance.

After a minute of dancing a slow dance, however, I saw there was a foreign-to-me hand in mine, that my skin was touching what seemed to be his much-different skin. Being that I'd grown up in the small desert community of Boulder City, Nevada, a strictly Caucasian community, and the few Black people I'd seen in Las Vegas had been at a distance until I enrolled in high school, I felt as though his skin against my olive/sallow-yellow skin, forget white, was a transgression. I was failing the code of acceptability.

I squirmed with efforts at small talk as I avoided his eyes— this nice, sensitive, handsome boy who'd asked me to dance. Too impressed, even encoded, with not-so-subterranean high school opinion, I'd caved. Miscegenation laws were still on the books in some states, banning some marriages. A breach of these laws was considered a felony with a prison sentence. Even if Nevada hadn't followed suit, these ideas had been carried like pollen through the air. I told him I wasn't feeling well and that I had to go home.

It was a lonely drive home. My dance partner was nicer than most of the boys I knew, smarter, more courteous. He was some- one I'd liked to have known, but I wasn't strong enough to buck the weight of public opinion I felt on my shoulders, even though no one had said a word. This "public opinion" was probably more the perception of a young girl with insufficient respect for herself. I perspired profusely as I drove. I felt empty as my hand that had touched his guided the steering wheel, drove me home to the edge of the desert. The world was an unfair place. I was party to the unfairness.

○

This morning as Bill and I drive the streets of Port Royal, I'm thinking of my ancestors who worked the land in Denmark, England, and Wales with their class systems, no change of caste allowed, though no one would have said that out loud. I'm wondering about the illusion of the so-called classless society in which we are now supposed to be living, in which being Black has often meant that one occupies a lower caste because of institutionalized racism. I'm feeling hapless in my own effort to bridge differences. I'm feeling contrite and low in spirit. I'm reaching my hand out. Somebody catch my hand.

We've been driving around in mostly silence for about fifteen minutes looking for a church to fit my specifications, when Bill spots a tiny white clapboard building. He brakes. A dark blue van is parked in front of a simply constructed church that needs a paint job. A man sits in the driver's seat behind a steering wheel. Another man sits on the passenger side. And there are others in the shadow of the back seat behind the tinted window glass.

"Is this what you're looking for?" Bill asks, the motor of our rental car idling.

"Sure," I say hesitantly.

"You don't sound too sure."

"No. This looks good." I swallow, the swallow sounding in my ears.

"If you'd like me to, I'll talk to the people in that van and see what's going on."

"That would be nice."

I am so obsessed with religion, spirituality, and the way people worship—God, Goddess, Father in Heaven, Yahweh, Allah, Jesus Christ, Buddha, Mohammed, Krishna, the Sun, the Moon, the Pope, Confucius, Lao-Tse, St. Francis and his birds, Mother Teresa, the Virgin of Guadalupe, Mary Baker Eddy, Joseph Smith, the Sufis, the Mystics. But I wonder if life itself is the only true church, the only true religion. It teaches us everything we need to know sooner or later. Maybe I don't need to keep looking.

But, bidden or not, I feel a sense of the divine even though divinity doesn't seem to be listening right now, not helping me right a wrong situation, or maybe it is and I just don't want to hear the answer. Whatever, whoever it is, God may be a name I've found along the way to make myself feel better. Maybe there's no He or She but something that transcends division. And yet, maybe there's no choice to be made for something I can't understand. But there's still Spirit I can feel when it's in the room. It's so big, powerful and undefinable.

In my passenger-side rearview mirror, I catch sight of a bent, dark gray woman walking toward the church, leaning on her cane that stabs the dust with each step. A shawl draped over her shoulders, she looks like Mother Time getting an eight-month start on the new year. She makes her way slowly to the steps of the church with its bare-spotted siding, puffs of dust rising with each dragging step.

Bill's back. He smiles as he slides under the steering wheel. "Surprise. The driver of the van is the pastor. He says you're welcome to join them. The service starts in fifteen minutes." He puts the transmission in drive. "We'll drive around before it starts. Okay with you?"

"What do you mean?" I say suddenly, the impact of his words sinking in. "*I'm* welcome to join them? I thought you wanted to do this with me."

"I've been thinking about it. You have respect for this kind of thing and at least you're a Christian. I'd only be an observer. Some kind of sociologist. That's not fair."

"But . . ."

"Think about it."

As I consider his words, I decide he's right. I can go into a chapel with strangers by myself, even though I'd have liked his company.

○

One basket a day. Six days a week.

A fanner basket was a winnowing tray, something like an inverted hubcap—a circular, barely curved bowl of a basket. A thresher tossed the threshed and pounded rice into the air. Up. Back down. Caught. Thrown up again until the wind heard the invitation from the sound of the rice rising and falling. Or until someone dropped rice into the fanner from a greater height.

But the wind still made its appearance. It carried chaff in an upward spiral, up and away from rice falling in midair. Rice and more rice until the bags were filled, until the wagons were filled, until the horses strained to pull the wagon to the docks.

One basket a day. Six days a week. Traditional weavers spent the Great Depression weaving sweetgrass, pine needles, and bulrush in Mt. Pleasant. "My [mother and sister] didn't have a clock. But the Greyhound bus would come through at midnight. That's when they'd stop and go to bed," Jeannette Lee recalled for Charleston's *Post and Courier.*

Early basket makers were men who made large baskets from bulrushes for storage and for carrying a row's worth of sturdy vegetables. Between growing seasons, they made baskets for plantation use and for sale by the plantation owners—a good basket, thus a valuable asset. Bulrushes being harder on the hands, the women who wove, and who were asked to weave more and more, found that sweetgrass was more pliable, softer, sweeter. They turned to delicate baskets for small uses such as bread, fruit, and storage of sewing supplies, socks, rings, and miscellany. The ripping of a blade of the stem of saw palmetto, the material used to tie the sweetgrass in coils, was and is their musical instrument, these daughters and granddaughters and great-granddaughters who still carry on the tradition begun in seventeenth-century America.

One basket a day. Six days a week. What will be placed in this basket? What will be brought and what will be taken away?

There's hope in the use of hands and in the smell and feel of sweetgrass.

○

We navigate a few more dusty roads, Bill and I. I've been haunting African American churches since back in the 1980s. I took a hiatus from the Church of Jesus Christ of Latter-day Saints and started attending other churches, starting with Calvary Baptist, in Salt Lake City. I'd always had a yen for the energy inside Black music and the sermons that made me feel alive and surging with that ineffable thing known as Spirit. Somehow, in the presence of African Americans, even though I don't claim their experience as my own, I felt my own soul rising inside of me, wanting expression, thinking it was safe to come out and show itself. I wanted to join the choir, wear a purple choir robe and sway down the aisle in procession. I wanted to give everything I had to the notes of the song, belt them out with no shame, nothing careful or prescribed. What I was used to sometimes felt like secondhand worship.

At Calvary Baptist, my eldest son and I sat next to an elderly woman in a purple net-covered hat and a green cloth coat. When Jonny gave her a big hug after France Davis, the pastor, asked us to greet our neighbors in the pews, she said to him, "We're not so different, you and me. We just got to get together." She held both of his hands in her small ones, her fingers as delicate as crocheted lace.

This morning, the inside of this church seems smaller than the outside. Two slightly dusty windows allow a share of morning light. A congregation of eighteen people, including five children, sit in sparsely populated rows. I sit by an older woman with a green pillbox hat and greet her with a handshake—the way Mormons greet each other in church. "I'm happy to be with you today," I say. Her hand shrinks back from mine. She doesn't seem eager for more conversation nor does she invite me to move any closer.

A young boy sits across the aisle staring at me—this tall, long-nosed, long-boned white woman with graying hair. I smile at him. He smiles back, then ducks his head. I get the impression I'm an alien sitting on the pew of his Sunday experience.

I hope a choir will appear soon, dressed in their long robes, swaying from side to side as they rock down the aisle, but nothing seems likely to appear from behind the speaker's stand. The more I assess these surroundings, this doesn't seem to be more than a one-room church with a small cloak room attached at the only side door I can see.

Just then, the minister appears from that door in his dark blue robes, the man who'd been in the driver's seat of the van. The sun's slant rays rest on the backs of the mostly empty pews.

"Welcome," he says, shyly at first, glancing my way. He seems somewhat timid or uncomfortable, and I sense I might be an intrusion on the regular doings of his Sunday mornings. "And we welcome our visitor. Let's all of us make her feel part of our worship today."

All heads turn in my direction, curious. There are small smiles of greeting, some nods of heads, and some lack of interest, which makes me feel like an intruder.

"We're low in numbers today which means we won't have a choir, sorry to say. Next week, Easter vacation being over, we'll be back in full swing. But, quiet now. Mama will now pray over us," he says, then stands back and folds his arms.

The aging woman I'd seen working her way toward church outside rises slowly, her hand resting on the back of the pew, her eyes closed and her head bent back to beseech the heavens. The room is absolutely quiet. The April sun is warming the panes of glass and the room. A spot of sunlight crosses the knees of myself and the woman next to me. A piece of reflected sunlight plays on Mama's eyeglasses. Refracted light dances on surfaces of pew backs and bent knees.

"I thank you for the lying down at night," she says, ever so slowly in a soft moan of a voice. Her hands are clasped in front of her. Long muscles extend at the sides of her neck, the tired ones that have been with her for a long time. Her voice sounds like the sea that carried her ancestors here on those slave ships. It has a slow, mournful sound of a language I don't know, a language with its own music. I imagine her voice as a deep melody from the Ancient Mother, the old whisper of wisdom rising up from the earth saying, "Here I am, my children. Been through hard times. I'm weary but I'm standing solid." The mournful yet grateful sound works its way through the layers of my skin, through my ears and mind. She's a lullaby I could listen to all day. She caresses each of us with her voice. We're beyond time.

"I thank you for the rising up in the morning," she continues. The word *rising* sounds like an actual rising up, a word stretched into flight, and I feel myself rising with the upward thrust of her voice before it falls again, slow, steady, more like the mellow waves that feather a shallow beach.

"I thank you for the blood that runs through my veins and gives me life." She sounds like a preacher herself, each word of her prayer an invocation and a blessing at the same time. Tears slip through my closed eyes. I've never thought to be grateful for the blood that runs through my veins, or for the rising up and the laying down—those too-simple things for which I never think to be thankful. Her powerful gratitude is woven into every syllable of every spoken word, even every space between the words.

My hand is all I have for a handkerchief. I can't hear the rest of what she says, her voice being so soft like the way we used to sing, "Swing low, sweet chariot," when I was a child, and yet, the hauntingly beautiful words touch me even without the full hearing.

Slaves. We've all been slaves to our fears, hurts, anger, jealousy

and greed, I think. Except the people in these pews are no metaphor. Their fathers and mothers have worn visible chains, and
I have no experience of that. They have felt the scorn of words
much darker than their skin. And here they are, giving thanks
while I'm crying—an ungrateful child among those who know
the inside-out of weeping until their tears have calcified.

At the end of the sermon, the minister calls the congregation to gather in a circle. He tells us to hold each other's hands.
I stand next to Mama and feel the flesh of her wiry hand. Delicate yet firm. Like the strands of sweetgrass tied together like a
cord, with strips of palmetto leaf. This is the hand of a healer, one
who has seen it all and can still forgive, one who can open her
arms and receive the least of her sisters. I feel her power through
my fingertips. I feel electricity coursing through my hands and
arms. A circle. An unbroken circle.

"God bless this sister who has visited with us today," the
minister says in closing prayer. "Bless her to know that God
lives, that Jesus will comfort her, that there's no way He brought
us this far to leave us."

When the circle finally breaks, I can't do more than say
"thank you" to Mama, my throat thick like it is, though I want to
put my arms around her weathered neck and kiss her cheek. She
looks at me from behind her thick glasses and I can see a place
of rest. Mama is the essence of this room, of this church, the
protector, the one who watches over it all as she strokes the back
of my hand. "Lead in the light," she says.

When I shake hands with the minister, I can't pretend my
face is dry. "Thank you for your sermon," I tell him, trying to collect my tears with my fingers. "And thank you for allowing me to
be with you today." He smiles kindly at my white woman's tears.

I walk out onto the small porch. Bill waits by the car.

"Thanks for finding this place," I tell him. "It was perfect.
Just what I'd hoped for, if I could just stop crying."

And yet, in 2002, as we drive back to our hotel past gigantic oaks draped with hanging, silvery moss and tall pines that seem to be leaning slightly as we pass beneath them, my tears dry with the wind from the open window. I suspect that real suffering is cheapened by tears, let alone mine. They are an element of the initiatory, the cleansing agent to clarify and purify, as sweetgrass is a purifier and a reminder that the earth provides. But these tears are not suffering in the deepest sense. It's time to stop crying and surrender like lilies of the field, toiling not, spinning not. As I look up at the top of one of those leaning pines with a halo of sunlight behind its top branches, I'm caught by a strong, fresh sense of believing I've come too far to be left alone.

○

It is night, and I'm walking outside our hotel room, walking across well-groomed grass on this barrier island with its tennis courts, golf courses, nature tours, bicycle paths to the beach and where sweetgrass had once grown wild and uninhibited. I walk just far enough not to worry Bill, whom I will divorce and then remarry eight years later, both of us coming to peace with our differences. I travel far enough away from the buildings and feel the sky overhead with its billion points of light. I think about catching the moon with a fish net, even catching a few stars, except if I reeled the moon in, there'd be no reflection from the sun, no light during the night for this planet where we live. I mustn't be selfish and want this soft moonlight all for myself.

I sniff the air. Maybe there's some sweetgrass nearby at the edge of the golf course, though people say most of it has disappeared with the development. It's said to smell like new-mown hay. It's said to be useful in entering a blissful, meditative state. Sweetgrass: the first plant to cover Mother Earth, according to native people of the Great Plains; the sweetness of knowing we're growing in the midst of other grasses; the sweetness of feeling our roots crossed under this marsh where we walk.

Responsibility:
The Essential Gesture

O

_/M_

"You can sing sweet and get the song sung, but to get to the third dimension, you have to sing rough, hurt the tune, then something else happens, the song gets large."

—Cathal

Y
ou could say it's useless to write in this world of too much information and where so many words could blow away in a strong wind. But, if the act is useful, which you believe it is, a person has a responsibility when putting words on paper—notably words meant for other eyes. Though it could be an unseen, unacknowledged responsibility, there's something that needs to be owned in the writing meant to be read by others.

You've always been a reader. Somewhere along the way, you developed the desire to write. Reading had given you an insight into other ways of being. Good literature transcended dualities. You wanted to make the difference you thought writing could make. You loved the big songs that pierced your heart. You believed in literature with a soul—the book that made you think, made you feel as though you'd been somewhere and experienced something, that you were a different person for having read those words. But maybe it would be better if your goal was to make a bundle of money and to entertain humorously with words. Simple. Straightforward. Anton Chekhov's words, "to describe a situation so truthfully . . . that the reader can no longer evade it," may not always be profitable.

But profit isn't the most valuable goal, even though you've secretly harbored a few wishes to be famous, to have the critics rave with admiration, and to have everyone read your work and thus make you wealthy. As a writer, you prefer wrangling with the tough places. It's part of who you are. It's your woof and weft. You care about fairness and justice. You care about people who are being ignored and treated as insignificant—"the deplorable masses." There's a keen responsibility for some things even if you're not totally aware of the reasons why.

Something that has been a major part of my own thinking has been my birth into a particular religion—the Church of Jesus Christ of Latter-day Saints, more commonly known as the Mormons. Some church leaders have expressed the idea that anyone who writes should promote the gospel of Jesus Christ: the sole purpose and goal of a writer's efforts. But what about the responsibility of writing something that contributes to a particular narrative other than the one experienced? It's challenging to differentiate between cultural mores, opinions, and theology. Furthermore, it's difficult to traverse the "Mormon" narrative, which, in the most generous terms, could mean the teachings of Christ and the building of the Kingdom of God—a place of higher compassion and ethics. This sounds good and beneficent, but the description is loaded because there are tendencies to be didactic, prescriptive, even moralistic at times, and to think this is the only or the supreme truth when there are so many ways of approaching the unknown.

Nobel Prize winner Nadine Gordimer writes in her essay, "The Essential Gesture":

one has only to watch very small children playing

together to see how the urge to influence, exact submission, defend dominance, gives away the presence of
natal human "sin" whose punishment is the burden of
responsibility . . . Responsibility is what awaits outside
the Eden of creativity. I should never have dreamt that
this most solitary and deeply marvelous of secrets—the
urge *to make* with words—would become a vocation for
which the world and that life-time ledger, conscionable
self-awareness, would claim the right to call me and all
my kind to account. The creative act is not pure.

You and I have "that life-time ledger, conscionable self-
awareness" calling us to account. We're aware of the *Lord of the
Flies* moments in our own childhoods when someone ruled the
playground with brute force, or the times we heard a peer taunt-
ing someone who was handicapped, disfigured, or "abnormal."
A person could be the brunt of bully mentality or, on the other
hand, could be a bully acting out of a sense of self-righteousness.
The dividing line might be thinner than we assume.

A sense of right and wrong can be a blunt instrument,
wielded without much awareness of the other side of the story.
To quote Rust Hills (fiction editor of *Esquire* from 1957-1964,
who championed such as E. Annie Proulx, John Cheever, and
William Styron, among others), from his article entitled "Moti-
vation": "If we are aware of a discrepancy between our own
horrid actions and our own nice selves, we can extend this realization to make a similar distinction between the behavior and
the self of another." We are people of paradox, people whose
shoes don't always match.

As for "conscionable self-awareness," there's something in
the observer, the writer, the conscience (with its notion of moral
goodness or blameworthiness) that affects our sense of responsibility. For instance, you might be a Valkyrie mother with iron
breastplates when your young children come home sobbing

because the bully had his or her way. But after you huff and puff with indignation and soothe the hurt that has become your own, you tell them to fight fire with fire. Or you take a position of passiveness, afraid or not wanting to show an aggressive face. You might find solace on higher moral ground, thinking yourself better than the bully while still and at the same time bullying others with your sense of justice.

Or, in another instance, you may have developed a fierce gut reaction to being pushed around or to watching someone else get pushed around. Maybe you've developed a crusader's sense of fairness. But you are not free of that natal human sin of which Gordimer speaks. Crusaders are capable of behaving badly on their side of the fence. They have their own demons to wrestle. You may be an advocate for the underdog because you grew up feeling *you* were the underdog. So, maybe you're merely taking care of yourself and your kind in an extended way and calling it compassion, goodness, or "conscionable self-awareness." Maybe you feel your own self-worth because of someone else's weakness. The ground is uncertain here.

If you want to write a fiction that matters, you need to examine the biases in your characters, which can only be understood after reflecting upon the biases in your own character. You, after all, are a human being. You need to look at those biases, especially in the writing of a non-fictive piece of work—a memoir or personal essay. There is an entire spectrum of possible behavior, not just the "goodhearted" or "vile villain" slices of the pie. Characters should not be less than three-dimensional if one is to matter as a commentator. A willingness to blast into the third dimension seems essential if one wants to sing those big songs or write those jagged, unpredictable stories with a *real* heart of gold.

In one of Gordimer's novels, *July's People*, Maureen and Bamford Smales are affluent, progressive liberals from Johannesburg. Raised with house servants, they nonetheless pride themselves on their broad-mindedness regarding racial issues in South Africa. After all, she and her husband have always been considerate to Black people, have been as gracious as they could be and provided their house servant, July, with "two sets of uniforms, khaki pants for rough housework, white drill for waiting at table, given Wednesdays and alternate Sundays free, allowed to have his friends visit him and his town woman to sleep with him in his room."

After a series of riots, arson, occupation of headquarters of international corporations, bombs in public buildings, gunned shopping malls, blazing unsold homes, and a chronic state of uprising in the country, the Smales are forced to flee Johannesburg with their two children to find refuge in the bush with their longtime servant, July.

Gradually, as Bamford and Maureen and children become more and more dependent on the people in the bush for their survival, a series of events forces Maureen into a different state of awareness. She begins to notice much of the shallowness of her former life in Johannesburg (the shallow repartee she had carried on with Bamford and the avoid-things-while-looking-good syndrome) and how inadequate it is in these new surroundings.

She realizes that this kind of repartee belongs to a certain "deviousness" that seems "natural to suburban life." When, in another instance, out in the bush, Maureen has to drown some kittens in a bucket and accepts it as a matter of course—a point-blank case of survival of the fittest—she realizes she and Bamford have been obsessed with the reduction of suffering but have given no thought about how to accept suffering. Bamford pities her that she should have to perform such an act, that she should have to suffer in that way. "Poor girl." He can't accept the fact that this is the best choice in the situation and that the natural cycle of life and death can be witnessed more clearly in primitive surroundings.

Finally, Maureen's shifting state of awareness gradually

evolves into a state of terror when she notices the shift of power to their former houseboy, July, whose territory they now inhabit because they have no place else to go. July not only has the keys to their car, but he drives it when he wants without asking permission. When July decides that the gun Bamford has for sport duly belongs to someone in the tribe who can use it for the greater good of the tribe, Maureen's terror escalates. Power is no longer in her hands—the woman with the precious white skin that has given her an elevated place in her particular life. Her husband is ineffectual in this close-to-nature setting; he can't pull the magic tricks he was used to pulling in civilization with his easy talk and trendy humor; his progressive ideas and habits seem merely laughable in the rawness of the bush country. The Smales are captives of those who were once their captive, no matter how graciously they perceived their servant, July, was kept.

Gordimer continually goes deeper and deeper into the layers of Maureen Smales's "conscionable self-awareness." The impetus for seeing her shallowness is the fact that the twisting, turning knife of power is now close to her throat and that she is at the mercy of the captor. Gordimer spares no one. She doesn't stop with the progressive white liberals and their easy phrases, simple assumptions, and what might be their unchallenged thinking. She shows the corrupting effect of power on whoever holds that power—Black or white. She probes behind the smiles and the glad handshake and the string of euphemisms of all her characters. Of what are humans capable?

Octavio Paz, the Mexican poet who won the Nobel Prize in 1990, says, "Social criticism begins with grammar and the reestablishing of meaning." There are real meanings of words such as charity, love, democracy—words that are bantered and tossed about freely. There are many things we say but many things we don't do. We talk about our fellow man and our neighbor but maybe we haven't thought about what that really means.

If you write to be read, you are answerable. "The creative

act is not pure." According to Gordimer, a writer has responsibility for various interpretations of the text; she is influenced by different concepts of morality: artistic, linguistic, ideological, national, political, religious. She needs to learn that her creative act is not pure even while being formed in her brain. Responsibility surrounded her at birth: genetics, environment, social mores of whatever class she inhabited, and the economic terms she was given when born.

One needs to look at her own essential gesture—what it is, what she cares about, and why anyone wants to hear about it. She needs to question the pearls of wisdom that were tossed in the air when she was young. Her parents implied that the unexamined life is not worth living. Or, they subtly taught that life should not be examined under any circumstances. Congenital burdens were placed on her, one way or another. Her idea of responsibility is part of her heritage, and her sense of responsibility could be a gut reaction to the things she's been taught.

Gordimer was born in the political hotbed of South Africa to Jewish emigrants from London. She experienced a typical European middle-class colonial childhood, the solitude of which was relieved by extensive and eclectic reading at the local library. She settled into her political awareness slowly, "sloughing off all the conditioning that you've had since you were a child." I hope it's possible to slough off my own conditioning in the hopes that I have a wide world to choose from where *everything* is sacred and worthy of the literary eye resting upon it.

As a writer, I have been shaped by the geography of the desert—the lonely, long stretches of what seems to be nothing; by the tenets, beliefs, and dogma of my particular religion; and by the teachings of my parents, those conservative, upstanding citizens. Knowing this, I still need to discover my own essential gesture. That is my work as a social being. I can choose to reach out to my cultural society alone, or I can put my hand out to society at large, believing that it's possible to build a bridge.

Gordimer writes of political things that address her South African culture, but her politics resonate with the universal. Her writing is not purely political (purely political writing can be purely bad writing, written to drive a point home or promote an ideology). She examines, probes, unearths the disparities in her culture and in its politics. This begs the question whether or not religious writing is a form of political writing. Maybe it's a writer's responsibility to distrust politics, literature, and even the way our heritage/theology is put together in our brains. If being a writer with a religious background means that one's writing should promote the Kingdom of God, does it also mean an unequivocal reverence for all things considered religious? It is a subjective word depending on whom you talk to. Maybe you need to deal with subjects such as homosexuality, pornography, infidelity, and sexual abuse without being seen as a traitor to the G-rated and harmonious life seen by many cultures as synonymous with goodness. Familiarity with or questioning of a suspicious subject does not automatically mean that a writer has fallen from the trajectory of white light.

You've accepted responsibilities given to you by your birthright and your rising from a particular geography and culture, but there is no such thing as "an average family" or "an average religious family." Some parents are devoted to their religion, but have a version of that religion in mind. They could be liberal or conservative in their thinking. They could be straitlaced Puritans. They could be bohemians.

My parents were compassionate people, very devoted to what they heard on Sundays at church, but they had their daily problems, one of which was living at the edge financially. They had to face the challenges of everyday life, even though they were shored up and strengthened at church on Sunday. My father wanted to be a writer. He moved every year of his growing-up life, was always the new kid in town, and his first friend was the librarian. He was a scrappy, sensitive, shy, intelligent kid, standing up for the underdog fiercely—sometimes to his detriment, sometimes done blindly. He never finished college. He talked about how he would have done so much better if he had. He stuck close to the church, as it gave his family some sense of continuity when his father vacillated between being a stable family man to one who couldn't keep a job because of his love affair with alcohol. To write about religion, for my father then, would be colored by the economic circumstances, his deeply conflicted father, and the unreliable environment in which he found himself as a young boy. There is a list of responsibilities he carried. How would he, as a writer, find his essential gesture—his gift back to society?

I have been affected by his scrappy sensitivity. I may have accepted every tenet my parents taught me, peacefully and graciously, with the hope of a rosy future. Or, on the other hand, I may have challenged my parents' certainty about the "right way to live." Maybe I saw them as putting me on a train on an infinite track with no windows or no doors and thus developed a fierce attachment to my right to question any and every thing.

Your writing life could be reaction. You could be a stubborn bull in a pen, snorting and pawing the ground, running in circles. You've concluded that your own particular responsibility is to move away from definition and be willing to see those things that might shock you. Rosa Burger, in Gordimer's *Burger's Daughter*, says that "freedom is to almost be a stranger to yourself." Maybe your responsibility is to see that the whole of who you think you are may not be the whole of who you actually are. Your conscionable self-awareness needs to see all facets of the crystal you call yourself. You also need to find those things you have that no one else has to give, that view of the world, that glimpse, that angle.

I hope my essential gesture includes a sense of compassion and a need for fairness toward all ways of being. This sensibility has been forged by the desert, my religion, my culture, my economic roots, and my parents, who had parents before them who may have been shaky citizens, proud pioneers, or denizens of the deep. I have that niggling feeling at the back of my mind that "I" is a drop of sand, a letter of the alphabet, a pronoun, an entity meant to surrender and to follow the Essential Essence so much wiser than the puny self. That thought stays with me and is part of the wild bird seed mix that comes out in my writing. But I can lift my experiences from their limited boundaries and transform them into a unique bloom of perception. There is still something left that is authentic to me.

Write what you feel bidden to write. Be ruthlessly honest with yourself about why you're saying what you say and how you say it. Italo Calvino—a renowned Italian writer of short stories and novels—says that literature and politics (and, I add, religion and even landscape), must above all know itself and *distrust* itself.

You can go beyond and behind the obvious. You can have that raw encounter with pristine creativity. Look in all the corners and let your imagination loose to play in the fields and meadows and even in the middle of the mean streets. Find your essential gesture, the responsibility you want to pass on, to convey, from the desk where you write.

ON BEING QUIET

O

In a dream, a friend of mine is telling a curious man in a bookstore about the books I've written. In her secretive way, as if she knows I'm overhearing, she's saying that the best one is titled *On Being Quiet*. Hmmm, I say to myself when I turn on my side and blink at the filtered morning light coming through the window. I haven't written a book by that name. This dream could be an omen or a harbinger notifying me of the need for inner peace, serenity, and a hushed mind.

The house is quiet. Children don't live here. Bill's still sleeping. No one is opening or closing doors or scraping a chair across the kitchen floor. Outside clouds block the sun. The morning seems like it's hardly happened yet. Cozy. Nonetheless, I ease out of bed, climb into the sleeves of my bathrobe hanging in the closet, and tie the belt. When I walk into the bathroom, there's a square of dim morning light next to my bare feet. This shape is mute, taciturn, except outside there are now raindrops on the roof playing havoc with the tin downspout.

I sit on the porcelain throne and think maybe this is the one time when people are closeted with quiet. There's usually no one to talk to, except for some who keep a cell phone with them at all times, who have a phone installed on the wall, or who always have something to read. You can hear pages turning or your stomach growling but generally the bathroom is a quiet place. As I sit, I look for patterns in the floor tile and think about what might have inspired someone to put such a concoction together: little painted pieces, simulated, supposed to make someone feel the exotic essence of old stone. I stare at door knobs, the smudge on the door frame and light switches, at the tub that could stand some scouring. But there's a pause between thoughts. There's only relative quiet here. I can still hear the rain and my mind is busy.

○

Something is always busy, even in the deep dark woods where people travel for solitude and quiet. They turn off busy freeways and leave congested streets behind and head to tall trees, ferns, those quiet things. But even there, industry is in full swing. The tiniest of creatures with multiple legs travel the length of a tree trunk or branch, or leaf, rustling, even on those tiny feet. The birds with their constant commentary are heedless of anyone seeking absolute quiet in their domain. So, I wonder, is it only "quiet" if everything is absolutely still and unmoving? Does it mean a storm is brewing? Outside? Inside? Or is that notion of quiet too extreme?

Life seems to be about noise, as much as I keep telling myself to be quiet so I can hear the largesse, that Great Silent Something existing somewhere outside the cavity of my head instead of those truck-driving thoughts that shift the gears on the freeway of my mind. Stillness. Silence. Quiet. Do they all mean the same thing? Maybe absolute quiet isn't a friendly thing. Maybe it has to do with death—the ultimate stillness.

I've seen total quiet—no noise, no unwanted sounds, but then, no response either. When I held my young hemophiliac son who had lapsed into a coma, I knew he was no longer with me. I didn't like being a witness. I wanted so much more then—a sign of life, of awareness, of movement.

Please, my baby, I begged. You're only three years old and the possessor of words and sentences. Please talk to me. Smile for me. Show me your beauty. Make those sounds with your tongue, with your lips, with the expressions on your face. You are part of the genealogy of bodies that have come before me. You are a strand of the twine that twists through the years and the bodies and all that has been. You are one of a long line of people, the ones whose names I know but whose story I do not, though I can guess at some of them or write fiction about them. All of what I can and can't see in your face must have appeared, to some degree, in the faces of those in our family tree, our ancestors, those who are quiet now and cannot tell us of their difficulties, their joys, their victories, their failures—the things they had to face, to do.

And I remember that night, eight hours later, with the help of respirators or anything else that might prolong his life, I yielded him to absolute quiet, no ifs, ands, or buts. To the place where he couldn't respond in the way I was used to having him respond. I'm not sure about the desirability of absolute quiet.

o

I set out on an eighteen-mile bike ride. I take a seat on a massive boulder. Looking out at the briny Great Salt Lake, I can see the remains of the second SaltAir that didn't survive—its brass onion dome bruises the blue of the late afternoon sky. I'm thinking about quiet, having left the city to find it. I thought it would be here. It isn't. Airplanes soar overhead, tractor trailer trucks roar past on I-80, seagulls screech, a train with cattle cars clacks around a bend.

A few things aren't making noise—the snow-topped Oquirrhs, the cloud reflections on the water, a fence that ends for no reason, two seagulls still as statues on top of a lamp post, the abandoned railroad cars daubed with yellow and white paint, the concrete barriers slumping into sand. A couple in the distance fixes dinner over a grill without talking. But then I hear other voices. How jarring that they should interrupt this reverie. People are barefoot at the lake's edge, squishing through mud. They're laughing. They're shouting. It's early spring. No snow-melt yet.

Is the world even supposed to be quiet? It seems as though there's always movement, something in motion. Even when I sleep with my ear to my pillow at night, I can hear my fingernail scratching on the other side. Like it's miked.

The once-serene seagulls on the top of the lamp post are squawking now because another seagull with webbed feet and a hooked beak much like their own is butting into their fraternity. The family Laridae is no longer a role model for quiet. And the people cooking their dinner: "Where is the catsup?" the woman says too loudly, her voice catching a wind current that flows past me.

Thinking about quiet interferes with quiet: the hum of a brain at work. Motion. Motion. Then rest between thoughts, but only temporarily. The mind at rest cannot stay at rest, at least while the heart and lungs are functional. Motion.

○

"A silent retreat?" I ask my friend who's been there before. "What is that?"

I attend a silent retreat in Crestone, Colorado, led by Sharon Landrith, an exceptional teacher who gives twice-a-day teach-ings. But the rest of us don't talk. We eat our three meals a day next to each other, but no one says a word. The gathering of the food, the mastication, the chewing, all done with no words, but it's not completely quiet. There is minimum noise in the kitchen—the pots and the pans, the whispering about whether or not this dish is ready yet. Then in the dining room: the sound of someone pulling back a chair, then sitting down with a tray in hand before placing it on the table. It's noisy, and yet we don't speak, even though one dinnertime I notice how a certain man is eating his quesadilla, somewhat differently from what the others are doing. One piece at a time. Broken apart. Small bites. And I think about manners and who taught us how to use them. Is there a right way to eat a quesadilla?

It's strange to pass another person without saying anything, without even smiling, but those are the rules here—as if we were walking alone among the bounty of the world, plentiful this time of year when flowers are still blooming and the harvest is ripe. The garden is a comforting place to visit after eating. The sun shines at a slant through the leaves of trees and bushes. After breakfast, I stand for at least fifteen minutes by the morning glories, the purple/red/yellow flowers that only bloom at first light of the day. They are maybe the most beautiful flower I've ever seen—their stamens, their petals, their colors—and I want to weep for the majesty of opening and closing that I don't usually notice or am even aware. So much happens when I'm looking the other way, busy talking.

Sometimes the exchange between people seems so much greater here. We aren't chattering or making talk just to make talk. The silence is pungent, turgid, full of itself, full of the meaning of all that isn't spoken. Becoming aware of this, I settle into the routine where we meditate for an hour before breakfast, between lunch and dinner, and after we listen to Sharon's dharma talks in the evening.

In one meditation, my son, who died over thirty years ago, speaks to me. My head is full of his voice, and I can picture him in all his innocence, too. "I love you, Mama," he says. That's all he says to me, but with what unbelievable power he has spoken. I weep again—first for the flowers, now my son. After all of my worry about his hemophilia when he was a young boy, after feeling guilty for making a body whose blood couldn't clot, after knowing I didn't know or do enough to care for such a child, he still loves me. I must remember. I must remember his words. His life and death has been a wound on my mind. I must forgive myself for my fear and guilt. And, for the first time, I think he knows, as I now know, that I love him, too. Love is by far the stronger response to his life.

When the attendees of the silent retreat speak again at the end of seven days, something is lost, some way of perceiving that can only be found when observing and listening. The talk seems mindless. Habitual. I can hear so much more in the silence.

○

Silence: (1) the condition or quality of being or keeping still and silent. (2) the absence of sound; stillness. (3) a period of time without speech or noise.

Quiet: (1) making little or no noise. (2) free of loud noise; hushed. (3) calm and unmoving. (4) free of turmoil and agitation; untroubled.

Still, silent, unmoving. Those words could speak of death.

Keeping still, the absence of sound, a period of time. This is the quiet I recognize.

○

I wake to the sound of my husband's deep, steady breathing. I'm reassured to know he sleeps peacefully; nothing is so healing as a good night's sleep. I snake out of our narrow bed, careful not to move the air mattress more than it needs to be moved, and then I open the door of our Vanagon. We've stopped as far away from public campgrounds as possible and parked next to an inlet of Lake Powell—another man-made lake in the desert. Reservoirs. Lakes. I can always tell that there's concrete or poured earth damming a river somewhere when there's so much blue covering the dust. It looks artificial even though I guess it's nice to have water in such a dry place—boats, fishing, water skiing, camping. The

sun will soon rise on the face of the water where mute canyons
are buried far below. I watch its changing colors and the progress
of light. Broad flat mesas still surface on this enormous collection of water and hold up the sky. I sit cross-legged in the sand,
pen in hand, notebook resting on my legs, and stare at the vista.
No hurry to record my thoughts that seem so small in this place.

A raven wings parallel to the horizon, displacing the air.
Even though the tumbleweeds pose as sleepers this morning,
yesterday they were racing through a noisy sandstorm. The pit-
ted sandstone of the cliffs seems blissful, as calm as a disciple of
Buddha, but there's overwhelming evidence it's been assaulted.
Pooled water has eroded its pocked face and created a poor com-
plexion. Wind has whistled, but now all is overpowering in its
silence.

The sun rises higher. Boats crisscross the water out in the
lake, bumping over the other's wake. One speed boat slows as it
enters the inlet where my husband, Bill, is now standing, fishing,
every move reflected in the water, arms raising, casting, falling,
without a sound. He's a profile in the morning sun, a picture of
tranquility, and the speed boat turns back to open waters.

The pen I've brought with me sits idle in my lap, as if to ask
why I'm bothering to make marks of any kind. A yellow and red
kayak slips through the water, the paddler unspeaking, silent.
Two people sit in camp chairs, watching, meditating on the
serenity of the long, flatliner horizon. Still. At rest. Even though
there is no visible heartbeat in motion, I sense a heartbeat
beneath this water and beneath this solidity in the core of molten earth—the earth always moving, its insides always ingesting,
excreting, or digesting something.

After no fish bite on Bill's line, we drive on an excursion to
a local restaurant for breakfast and then explore several roads
to nowhere. Stirring up billowing dust behind our camper, we
follow well-worn tire tracks until it appears that someone gave
up on making this a road to somewhere. Too iffy to keep going.

Bill says it's time to turn back. "Why get stuck in the middle of nowhere?" he says. "No one in sight, only mounds of red sand, bushes, and distant mountains?" Even though we're here early before the summer vacationers invade every nook and cranny, we're here at the beginning of the week. Out of sight of everyone and everything civilized may not be a good thing since we're not geared up in a four-wheel drive with monster tires, nor do we want to be.

"This used to be the middle of nowhere," I respond as Bill turns the Vanagon around. "Miles of desert and red rock. Arches. Imagine how quiet it must have been then."

By the end of the day, after we've eaten the dinner I prepare on the camp stove, the water of the lake is as flat as glass. There's a long line of stilled houseboats barely moving, as if they're glued to that surface. Fingers of rock jut out into the water. Even longer fingers of water reach back, past the stone embankments: a clasp of sorts, fingers interlacing with fingers. Crickets rub their legs together, singing, who knows what they're doing, but it's a sound of summer. The luminescent blue of the silky water reflects the red stone.

As the red-tinted sky prepares to drop the sun behind the mountains, which makes me think of basketball, I listen to the sound of feet walking up the dirt road, crunching sandstone gravel, and the bang of the metal door in the campsite bathroom. Someone sings a nasal, hillbilly song, but then the sun sinks away in this great escape, this road away from civilization, and a scepter moon appears. At first, we can hear the unwelcome sound of generators for motor homes where the occupants watch television or recharge their refrigerator. Why do we even bother to go to the Great Outdoors, I'm wondering. It's not quiet here. But thank goodness for the rule that generators have to be off by ten o'clock. Soon, those sounds die out, and the campsite is mostly quiet. Latecomers pitch a tent in the campground, their sometimes-soft voices deciding where to stake and what will hold. Someone strums a guitar at a neighboring campfire.

Maybe the only way I can find quiet is to practice Zen meditation and find it within myself. In today's world there are always infringements—airplanes overhead or trucks on the nearest interstate or rushing traffic, even the murmuring of a narrow stream running down to the lake or of something digging a hole beneath the branches and leaves of a nearby bush.

But now, it's quiet here by the big human-made Lake Powell where so many people gather to get away and find serenity. Once, there were very few people who ventured into this high desert territory inhabited by loners of the reptilian variety and a few coyotes. But now, bodies are settling in. The soft voices. My husband's pencil writing in the numbers for a Sudoku puzzle by the light of a kerosene lamp. But the star peeking through the clouds is so bright it seems noisy, as if it's shouting like crazy some zillions of miles away, fireworks and gasses erupting everywhere and we think they're so silent, static. Twinkle, twinkle.

○

I don't think I'm ready to write that book—*On Being Quiet*. I'm not sure I've thought about quiet enough, but maybe my friend has been trying to tell me something I need to know.

Maybe. Maybe not. In silence one can still feel the wind on one's arms and back of the neck and know that things are moving and happening. But now, returning to the desert and the lake, I wonder about how soundless quiet needs to be. A duck floats on the water, which is rippling again, making small noises. There's a muffled sound of a plane high overhead and its contrails are spreading thin in the sky. A fishing boat is plowing the waters. Countless thousands of sandstone rocks and slabs must have clattered immensely in the rains and slides and quakes. There's a gentle burble of birds in a bush, a fly passing by, the flapping of an overhead bird's wings. These things help the stillness feel restful, even more still, but maybe we're trained to listen for interruptions of the silence, rather than for silence itself. Maybe because silence feels too empty, too full of echoes, or the thought of a grave.

Maybe stillness is movement at rest: hardened tire tracks in sand, a yellow tent tucked into a crevice in the rocks, strewn sandstone boulders, broken pieces of shell, gnome stones, sage-colored mushroom hills. But then everything begins again and again. Moving. Participating in the silent void. Consider the voiceless lizard doing push-ups on slant rock, the new green growing in an unlikely place, a bird floating on an unseen draft with wings extended. And fingers of blue water inching up the sides of islands as spring runoff comes to the lake. Alive.

THE NESTED SELF

n Russia, there's a popular folk art which is the carving and painting of the nesting doll known as matryoshka. *One of these dolls sits on my desk. Painted in shades of green, she's wearing an elaborately detailed babushka that covers most of her red hair. She has piercing green eyes and a delicate face, and a winter scene is painted across the front of her in lieu of a dress. Through the ages, people everywhere have been fascinated with taking these dolls apart, splitting them open and open again to smaller and smaller versions until reaching the doll that no longer breaks apart. Perhaps people see something of themselves in these dolls, something about removing layers or breaking one's self open to the mystery of their core, their essential "I."*

That matryoshka is sitting on my desk, prim, proper, gilded in gold paint, closed up tight for now. In my sitting-and-staring-into-space moments, she causes me to wonder how many selves are nested in this thing called the self. I have many assumptions about who I am encased in my flesh, though luckily, human flesh is not so brittle and hard as the shell of this doll. Some of my memories, however, make me sad. How could I have done this or that? I've made some conclusions that gnaw at strange hours.

But maybe I've approached the subject of me from a limited rather than full-throated angle.

My mind playing with the contours of this doll sitting in front of me, I can't help but wonder how the idea of matryoshka affects my writing.

My book *Raw Edges* started out as a novel about the adventures of two women bicycling across the United States. A chick novel. I could make money! A year later, it veered toward being a novel about two women bicycling across the US trying to unburden themselves of their guilt and personal failure. Another year later, the text informed me it was more memoir than novel. It was about me taking an insane bicycle trip because my own life had seemed so inconsequential at the time. I'd lost track of my reasons for being. On closer inspection, I saw lurking beneath the surface of my get-rich, be-famous novelistic intentions—like a Loch Ness monster—this looming personal guilt that kept rising from dark waters to haunt me.

I wasn't sure what to do. Perhaps I should go for the jugular and tell the rawest truth I knew. Pull back the curtain and say, "It's me here. I'm the source." Or I could keep the curtain drawn and pretend I wasn't on the stage. I could write a *memovel* or a *novoir*.

Contradictory strands of advice were woven into the braid of this dilemma. As a young girl, I'd been advised not to talk about myself too much, and yet I was also told that "the truth shall set you free." These notions and others like them created such a stark duality that I felt torn in two directions: (1) toward a truth that needed to be told and (2) away from a truth that shouldn't. I felt I was two people: this person called "I" whom I'm not supposed to mention, and this person called "I" who must be examined. Other writers have solved this dilemma by turning to fiction. Some are compelled to write in first person and tell it "like it is."

I was taught to tell the exquisite truth at all times. That virtue was hammered into me as a child: I must be the honest, double square, full-of-integrity person whose every word is truth. Therefore, I felt compelled to confront the truth, to face the guilt I'd been suppressing. I felt like Laurie Alberts, my colleague in the Vermont College of Fine Arts writing program, who says in her memoir *Fault Line*, "I have no right to fiction's veils and masks. They keep me too safe. In the fan dance that is fiction, I can play peekaboo with the truth, be coy, expose myself just so much, then deny everything." The truth, I decided, was more important than my safety.

But what could I gain by using memoir as my base of operation?

Possibly, no-holds-barred writing could touch closer to the truth, to the essence of what it means to be an individual human being here on this earth. "This is me. I'm standing naked in front of you. What you see is what you get." I didn't want to wander through the labyrinth of illusion, fabricating stories. I wanted to present a unique self and a time and place to be received as is. Unconsciously, I had come to think of this kind of writing as the only kind that mattered. It was the place to which I naturally gravitated.

o

I pause now to open the nesting doll in my hand. Inside is the second version of the painted woman with a golden babushka covering all but one lock of her red hair. Another winter scene—a snow-packed road to a snowed-in house—is painted across the front of her body.

Before I had much advanced education in writing, I wrote for several magazines and journals in Salt Lake City, Utah. My first submission to *Utah Holiday* was a personal essay entitled, "Confessions of a Snowplow Queen," followed by "What Does a

Nice Girl Like Me Get Out of Belly Dancing?" and "How to Plan Your Own Funeral" (written after the death of my three-year-old son). Among others, "How I Raised a Rock and Roll Band and Learned to Write" appeared in *Salt Lake Magazine*, and "The Precarious Walk Away from Mormonism, All the Time with a Stitch in My Side" appeared in *Dialogue: A Journal of Mormon Thought*. It seemed I wanted to write out my angst, put it on paper to better understand and, bonus-time, share it with readers. I found I could tell soulful stories and gather readers in my net.

I did, however, stretch myself, trying my hand at a broad range of nonfiction writing. I experimented with investigative journalism, feature articles, reportorial articles, impersonal essays, and book reviews. But, just before publication of my most notable investigative reporting article, titled "Culture Shock," an award-winning piece later anthologized in *A World We Thought We Knew: Readings in Utah History*, the editor of *Utah Holiday* received a letter from a reader who said something to the effect of, "I'm tired of reading about Phyllis Barber. Why don't you get her to write about something more than herself?" The tone of her letter was something like, "How dare she be so intimate with us about her life?" The editor thought the letter was mean-spirited and off the mark and was also aware that the substantial investigative reporting article was coming out in the next issue. He chose not to publish the letter but I did take note. It could be totally indulgent to think other people wanted to hear about my life.

Except, maybe all our lives are ultimately the same, especially in their contours, granted that there are variations in perception and the way our stories get told. Total honesty could contribute, being that not everyone was a writer. It could pierce another person's unwillingness to examine the mask they might be wearing.

○

I pull the next doll apart to reveal the smaller version inside, still with the same golden babushka and red shock of hair in the middle of her forehead. She's getting smaller, possibly more intense. She's still painted beautifully in the same green paint and with the same lacy embellishments, but a different house on a different snowy road covers her chest.

I enrolled at the University of Utah to elevate myself and my writing, to aspire to the realm of *artiste*. After writing a year's worth of experimental fiction, I began a series of stories about growing up Mormon in Las Vegas. I fictionalized the names, exaggerated the characters somewhat, invented things that would make for a better story, and proceeded to put together a book of short stories. But people who read them said, "These sound like autobiography. This is memoir." Even though I was bound and determined to be a writer of fiction, much of it seemed less direct and more like impressionistic music than story. My nonfiction had a directness that hit home.

Finally, I decided to enter the Associated Writing Programs' annual writing competition in creative nonfiction. Before submitting the manuscript in its "fictional" form, though it was really a memoir, I wrote a letter seeking permission. The judges said that wouldn't be a problem, but that if I won the contest, I would have to change the names to the real ones and own up to its close-to-the-boneness. When I won that year, I did just that. I took refuge and solace in the words *creative* nonfiction because I had taken creative license. I'd drawn these events from a cloudy, even fog-bound memory and put my own spin on it, and if you consulted with my sister, she might tell you a different story.

I became suspicious about the word *I*, about the possibility of telling *the truth* in personal essay or memoir. In my younger days, I believed if I dug deep enough into the self, I could find answers about who I was, but the authentic self is much more elusive and challenging to locate than one might imagine. I'd been creating my own legend, my own myth, my own explanation of myself to myself. I needed to ask the tough question, "How well do I see what I think I see and how accurately do I interpret what I see?" There might be someone known as "I" making up a lot of stories to entertain herself.

○

Again, I break open the matryoshka *in my hands. Tinier still, the fourth version of the doll appears the same, but the details of her face are slightly altered by the smaller scale of the diminished surface. Her winter scene is composed of snow-covered trees by a frozen stream. Has the doll changed by being opened up?*

I began to ponder tough questions. I wondered.

We tell a particular story. One could tell a story about him or herself to get more attention (e.g., poor me, I'm such a delicate creature I need to be handled with kid gloves. Or, I am the Queen of Something Somewhere, so give me my due). Our stories could be based on the kind of stories people will listen to. We are survivors. Literature, or storytelling, is necessary to survival. Whoever makes up the best, worst, or saddest story wins.

We tell stories to justify ourselves to others. I can say, "If only everyone understood me then they would love me." I can say, "I only did this because of that," and you would believe me.

A story, by nature, gathers bits and pieces of chaos and orders them into a narrative. Fragments are selected from chaos and that implies the act of creating fiction. An entire life can't be told in a memoir or in any written text because that means 24-7 of mostly insignificant detail. And there are those sleeping hours.

When we put together the story of ourselves, there are objective, freestanding facts. But then, these events are laced together and seen through a particular angle, which may be different from what actually happened. The "I" arrives at a truth of its experience, but maybe this truth is fiction. Writers and people in general could well be stuck in the notion of who and what the "I" is. The "I" that I want to talk about could be a subjective entity, and subjectivity implies imagination. Yes, there are facts, but maybe it's impossible to have a definitive stance when it comes to the difference between truth and fiction.

Even as I think these things, I'm aware that the person I refer to as "I," me, this woman writing to you, is a complex entity. I've been many people. Once I was Phyllis Nelson, good Mormon girl with raven-black hair, who desired to be a good mother and wife and concert pianist more than anything else. (As I stand back from this description to take notice of the words I've chosen to tell my story—"raven-black hair," "good mother," "concert pianist"—I see I've chosen them for dramatic effect.)

And there was a time when Phyllis Nelson wanted to be a Las Vegas showgirl, a high-fashion model, and an assistant to the Nevada senator in DC (I stand back again to confess these were only three of many options that occurred to me during the wild fervor of my youth, but I chose the jazzier selections). I was also Phlea—nicknamed as such because I probably seemed to hop from one thing to another.

Another time I was Phyllis Barber, a not-so-black-haired fiery rebel, community volunteer turned restless artist, belly dancer, a woman chomping at the bit to be recognized in the world of the arts, wanting to make a significant contribution. And then there is the moment when I am Phyllis Barber-Traeger, older woman with gray hair, a sympathetic face, and a new husband. But appearances may be deceiving. Maybe I'm a wise, distinguished older woman, but I still have frightened teenage elements in this woman's body. I'm a different "I" today from the one I was yesterday. I am everything I ever was.

There is an essential "I" that is still me when all the trappings fall away, but maybe it's only a skeleton. "I" could outlive its own flesh. The "I" inside could be an eternal entity—a spirit. The "I" could be about something apart from a squirrel-cage mind and body.

○

As I break open the matryoshka *once again, I find the fifth doll is very small, but there's still a crack in the middle, which means there's at least one more inside. Her expression is less serene than that worn by her predecessors.*

How many selves are nested in the "I"? Here are five renditions of what might be the truth of the full-metal-jacket guilt I've been wearing for thirty-plus years now:

I had a hemophiliac son who died of a cerebral hemorrhage when he was three years old. The doctor, who had seen him two days before his death for a routine checkup, wasn't sure why he died. But a hemophiliac can step off a curb and start bleeding internally. My son had a bad cough. This was the cause.

I had a hemophiliac son who died. I may have snapped him on the forehead with my fingers when he was being impossibly unruly on a difficult morning. I can't remember for sure.

I had a hemophiliac son who died of a cerebral hemorrhage. The day before he died, I snapped him on the head, a snap of my fingers against his temple. I caused my son's death.

I had a hemophiliac son who died. I'm not sure what caused his death, but I've been racked with guilt ever since. I always felt guilty about giving birth to a handicapped child. It follows that I would feel guilty about his death.

I suspect myself of loving the tragedy of life. It is true that I don't know what happened. I DO NOT KNOW.

○

The Zen master Dōgen says:

> To study the way is to study the self.
> To study the self is to forget the self.
> To forget the self is to be awakened with all things.

I come to this page with a religious-spiritual background,

and the words of the Zen master speak to me in my wondering about the "I" and how much of that "I" has been created by my imagination to wrangle random details into a story. Perhaps my susceptibility has to do with a quote, purportedly from Willa Cather: "Artistic growth is, more than anything else, a refining of the sense of truthfulness. The stupid believe that to be truthful is easy; only the artist, the great artist, knows how difficult it is." But what kept me going all those years when I continued to fall back into writing things I knew and felt guilty about (as though I were insufficient because I couldn't create something greater than or apart from myself) was the conviction that if I dug deeply enough and told of my barest, rawest, most difficult encounters with this business of rollercoastering up and down the days, I would be telling "everyone's story." I would be freeing myself. I would be freeing others.

The irony is that the deeper I dug into my own being, the less I seemed to know my core. In fact, the more I tried to pin myself down, the more evasive the "I" became. On some days, "I" was impulsive, loving, generous, noble, tender, caring, while on other days, "I" was greedy, biased, selfish, hopeless, etc. The self was much more slippery than I'd imagined. It was like mercury—if you were unfortunate enough to play with it before it was deemed poisonous, highly toxic, and lethal—how when you touch it, it bends away from the touch. Mercury is literally "non-gatherable," for want of a more scientific word.

○

At last, as I disassemble the doll, no further disassembling possible, I find the tiniest carving. She's a hard, little thing, and yet she doesn't feel like a core, which I would imagine to be more like the molten center of the earth. She feels like the craftsperson had to stop because it was too difficult to break this small thing into two halves. Her expression is inscrutable. A mystery.

Some philosophers and esoteric teachers believe that the "I" is only a construct of language. Maurice Nicoll, an English psychiatrist instrumental in explicating the ideas of G. I. Gurdjieff and P. D. Ouspensky, says in one of his books:

> The idea . . . is that just as we can change our position in the outer world by physical effort, so we can change our position in the inner world by psychological effort. . . . Each of us has a psychology. . . . At any moment you are somewhere physically and somewhere psychologically. Outer observation shews you where you are physically; inner observation—that is, self-observation—shews you where you are psychologically. To be in a bad state psychologically is as if you might be in a dark corner of a room, sitting there, morose and gloomy, when you might shift your position easily and stand in the light. . . . Self-observation . . . is to make us aware of where we are *psychologically* at any moment and eventually to shift our position. *Where we are* psychologically at any moment is *what we are at that moment, unless we are aware of it and separate internally from it.*

Every day, hour, even minute, the "I" goes through changes of psychological states. The individual is in a passenger car, riding through the changing landscape of boredom, stress, worry, anxiety, inferiority and superiority. When you say, "I am a loser," for instance, you are not speaking of a permanent condition. You may be a loser for an hour and something else in the next. "I am brilliant," is the same thing. "I am a great writer. I am a poor writer." The "I" can be all of these things at different times. But a psychological state is not the "I." It is a psychological state. Nothing more. Nothing less.

Nicoll says further that "if you cannot admit that you have a *psychology* at all and say 'I' to every state it leads you into, you can get nowhere."

Maybe there's not one unified I, but rather a collection of I's, as Gurdjieff suggests. When we use the term "I," we could be referring to a particular psychological state—"I'm bored," "I'm angry," "I'm no good"—which is not consistent or permanent. Or we could be referring to a particular physical state—"I'm tired," "I'm old," "I'm young"—which is also not consistent or permanent.

The Buddhists speak of the principle of the not-self as a means of opening the path to enlightenment. According to Thich Nhat Hanh, a Vietnamese poet and Buddhist teacher, "Not-self signifies absence of permanent identity. Not-self is impermanence itself. Everything is constantly changing. Therefore, nothing can be fixed in its identity. Everything is subject to not-self."

While thinking about this essay, I went to the dentist's office, where she gave me a healthy dose of nitrous oxide (I told this dentist that "Just Say NO" really means "Just Say Nitrous Oxide"). Under the influence, I had a vision. It was about how human beings are much like blades of grass in a field. They distinguish themselves, trying to be bigger or smaller than the next blade, richer or poorer, smarter or dumber, more sophisticated or less, but basically, human beings are all blades of grass, tied into the same natural order of things, the same nutrition, the same finite limitations.

Other analogies move closer to the mystical: each individual is a drop of water in the Ocean of God, or, as the Hindus say, everyone is a cell on the body of God. Maybe we are all slivers or moods of the Great I Am. Maybe we are water in the river. When we say, "I Am," might we be referring to Higher Power or the Divine Essence or to Something Beyond Our Understanding? Maybe "I Am" can never be contained in one human body, or maybe it is all there in all of us.

When we take a childhood memory—say, a memory of being criticized for being too thin-skinned—and commit it to paper, we also commit ourselves to one idea of who we once were. We have closed off other options about who that child might have been.

My contention, as should be clear by now, is that when you sit down to write a personal essay, memoir, autobiography, or even an intimate, thinly disguised novel, you are just as inventive with the creation of the "I" character as you are with any fictional character. You select fragments of yourself to support a thesis, much as a scientist uses various scraps of evidence to prove a particular theory.

A story is a creation. The life you live is intrinsically related to your perceptions about it. You may be so busy telling the story you've told a thousand times that you're unable to disentangle from the threads of the story you've invented to explain yourself to yourself. You've come to believe the story you've created. You've closed your mind.

It's possible that you've created a particular story in order to matter in the scheme of things. For example: I'm from more than the desert, I'm more than the mother of a hemophiliac child who died, more than a Mormon girl who's struggled with orthodoxy. There are other stories to tell than the ones I'm accustomed to telling. I want the reader's sympathy but need to ask whether or not I'm willing to challenge my own stories about myself. I need to take a deeper look, even with the knowledge that I may never arrive.

One's personal history is inextricable from one's writing life however it manifests itself. You can't have one without the other, though I guess you could get rid of the writer. I've come to believe in allowing our oft-told tales some breathing room. Only when you accept that the self is a mystery, not something that can be pinned down like a dead butterfly, is change possible. *Novoir* might be the best word to describe the process.

I quote Hafiz, a thirteenth-century Persian poet, slightly adapting one line:

I have a thousand brilliant lies
For the question:
[Who] are you?

I have a thousand brilliant lies
For the question:
What is God?

If you think that the Truth can be known
From words,
If you think that the Sun and the Ocean
Can pass through that tiny opening
Called the mouth,

O someone should start laughing!
Someone should start wildly Laughing—
Now!

THE DESERT, AGAIN

Here I am again, thinking about the Mojave Desert. I'm wondering about memory and about the places everyone turns to when they indulge in these memories. It comes as no surprise that I turn to the desert. I've been here before. Many times.

I'm walking through the sand and the sage, ol' Sol pouring down on my head, my back and shoulders, my whole body feeling the grip of the sun. I'm thinking about my childhood, about living in Boulder City next to the Hoover Dam, and then moving to Las Vegas. I'm wondering what makes a person who she or he is. I'm thinking about how one "becomes." All of this is intertwined and intermixed in the head beneath my hat. There are many clues for me here in Clark County, in southern Nevada, in this desert.

It seems I'll always be walking through the sand and always reliving the details of my young life. I can feel the gentle breeze before the sun starts to roar. Creatures of the desert hide from my sandaled feet as I wander from hole to hole, wondering who lives there. A rat? A snake? Something else? Sand fills my shoes:

hot grains trickling into the place where my heels are supposed to be cushioned, tiny pieces sneaking past the laces and sticking to the space between my toes—toe jam, we call it. And then there's the cactus. It warns me to keep my distance or suffer from its prickly needles that stick out every which way.

As I'm walking through my memories, I remember the time I fell from my bicycle. My father found it at the city dump, a bike with balloon tires, its dented fenders painted black to cover the scrapes. On that particular day, my tire slipped on the dirt road that wound into the desert. The bike went straight out from beneath me, slanting sideways, tilting, crashing to the ground. I tumbled. All askew. Knees and arms mixed up. I scraped the skin from my thighs big time. Blood and gravel tangled together until I couldn't tell what was my leg and what was the desert. Only a memory of skin, that's what it was. Two unrecognizable thighs. Mutilated. Maimed, and I cringed at the thought of Mercurochrome, my mother's favorite remedy for cuts and abrasions. It would sting when she painted it over my big owie. She could be ruthless when it came to wounds.

I limped back from the open desert to Boulder City, back to our pleasant home trimmed with a green lawn and red shutters, a house bought in Henderson for $4,000 and brought on a trailer to rest at 616 Fifth Street. As I had dreaded, my mother painted my thighs with Mercurochrome. I cried, probably for longer than I needed to, but the pain was bad.

Nonetheless, Boulder City was an idyllic town, a creation of the Department of the Interior, the Bureau of Reclamation, and the Six Companies—the combination of companies pieced together to build Hoover Dam. It was built to house the worker bees as well as the overseers, cooler than Las Vegas and less prone to the wiles of men. The government made all of the rules in this town and designated it as a reservation, this oasis in a hostile desert. One could almost smell the town's respectability and the smooth-running federal government at work, though, it should be noted, this kind of town was an oddity in the wind-blown state of Nevada.

When the dam was being built, one had to pass through a guarded gate to enter. On weekends, some men went out of the reservation borders to Railroad Pass if they wanted a drink, entertainment, and a chance at mixing with a single woman. But during the week, there were strict rules. It was too dangerous to work on the dam if one was impaired in any way. In the early days, my grandfather was the greengrocer at the commissary, my uncle was an electrician at the evolving dam, and my father drove trucks full of gravel before he became the secretary for the city manager, Sims Ely.

The dam was ultimately finished—a stronghold that would withstand the years and would prove to be more impregnable than the water itself. And, of course, our grandmother sang at its dedication. I wish I knew what she sang.

I was born in 1943 (the dam was dedicated in 1936), and, daily, we heard about the powerful and sturdy dam. It ordered our lives. The Bureau of Reclamation presided over the town, housed in a strong, concrete building at the top of the highest hill. It was a city landmark. Our family used to picnic on its front lawn beneath its serious windows. After we finished our sand-wiches and fruit punch, we kids rolled down the steep slope as fast as possible. The town held an annual Easter egg hunt there, and I always hoped I could find one of the baskets with the gold-foil chocolate egg. It was best to be one of the fast and savvy searchers. It helped to have scoped out the pickings beforehand.

In this solid town, we, the children, went to Boulder City Elementary in a concrete building, a fortress even, because every building of importance was built from the concrete readily avail-able from the dam site. Like most kids, we ate meatloaf, went to church, practiced the piano, laughed, slammed doors, slept outside on hot nights, played Monopoly, Clue, and checkers, entered spelling bees, and ate apricots from our tree before they fell to the ground. We used to keep some of the overflow tourists from Las Vegas when the Chamber of Commerce called, asking if we wanted to house someone for the weekend. That was our chance to bring in a tidy sum of money, which we could always use. And we often took them to the dam to see its innards—the generators, the intake towers, the dripping water over one of the diversion tunnels. In Boulder City, there was sense and sensibility to our lives.

But then, in 1954, when I was in sixth grade, our family moved to Las Vegas, its Spanish name meaning "The Meadows." We moved into a tract home across the street from another desert, and our solid world began to blur at the edges. Landing there felt like being shot onto the barren surface of the moon. It was too hot, inhospitable, and a harsh place. The walls of our home barely stood up to the wind when it blew. We tried to make our lives as solid as a life could be, given the nasty-tasting water in our taps, given that it was a dusty wasteland with no water left in the Springs, the water which had originally tempted people to settle there.

The desert across the street from our house seemed hotter and less inviting than the one in Boulder City. More windblown. Scrappy. Unfriendly. I felt no invitation to wander there. Maybe I was older and wiser, or maybe the desert seemed more forbidding. I had to deal with limp hair, dust on the windowsill, and dripping perspiration from my underarms to my waist. I'd graduated to a harsher terrain.

My psychology of life was formulated here and stamped indelibly by our move from stability to windblown chaos, our father making promises of a better life and then struggling to deliver, the town feeling less than one piece.

At the time, Las Vegas was a flat, thrown-together, no-account, wannabe-reputable town built in wide-open spaces. Its rough-and-ready businesses and bars were jerry-rigged together at the side of Boulder Highway. Most of its tacky houses were built on top of sand, no basements. They belonged to no one, not really. Paper thin, too shabby, trees planted all around to make them look permanent.

I wanted to belong here but this town and desert didn't protect me or my family the way our well-ordered government town in Boulder City had. My father's work was not as profitable as he had hoped. The Las Vegas insurance agents were more aggressive than he was used to being and not as interested in quality over quantity. It seemed as if all of our family was taken down a notch or two from the respectability and civility we'd known.

Over a few years of trying to make it in this ragtag place, a strong desire kidnapped my rational thinking. I would matter here, somehow. No one would stop me or say I wasn't good enough, even if I had the perfunctory acne and poor posture of a girl grown too tall too soon. I wished on stars and dreamed dreams. I learned to do the splits so that I could kick high and become a Las Vegas Rhythmette—the precision dance team from Las Vegas High School. That success was something I considered a coup de grace, a conquering blow to end any misery I might have. Secretly, I dreamed even more vivid dreams of becoming a showgirl wearing over-sized sunglasses and posing for a photographer on the end of a diving board, my cleavage abundant and my tiny waist encircled with a gold chain. I also visualized my parents in a long, pink Cadillac with me in the back seat wearing rhinestone sunglasses. This was Las Vegas, after all. New terrain.

But the desert across the street offered no hope to sensible minds. There were no creeks or stands of green trees, unbelievably hot sun, and cagey creatures that were scaly, stringy, and ropey, even if I hid indoors with a swamp cooler and read biographies with predictable orange and beige covers from the library. That wasteland was always out there waiting. I couldn't escape it. I was a child of this unfruitful, infertile, sterile place.

And yet . . .

While the desert isn't exactly friendly, I've always been

drawn to it like filings to a magnet. No matter what else happens in my life, it still remains embedded beneath my skin, just as it was when I tipped over on that black bike my father fixed up for me. The desert is caught somewhere in my body. Maybe it never went away. The heat. The wind. The sand. It's all there.

The desert is subtle. It lies behind the façade of what men have tried to build. It tries to send people away with its bitter wind and searing sun. But it has taught me to find my way through, to accept me, whether or not I'm beige, the color of sand, if that's what I am. Quiet. Reserved. I'm a creature who has found a way to live in the midst of challenges. My response is not easy to track. I could be the desert itself.

It's true that we are all part of other places we've lived, in my case the Bay Area of California; Salt Lake City and Park City, Utah; Denver, Colorado; Rochester, Minnesota; and the many places I've traveled—Arkansas, South Carolina, Tibet, India, Iceland, Spain, England, Ecuador, etc. But a large part of who I am will always be a metaphor: a piece of sand warmed by the sun. How I love to be warmed by the sun, especially when it doesn't burn too hot.

Though it took years to come to peace with my childhood and put my geography in perspective (even while Las Vegas became different from what I'd known), I've discovered that it doesn't matter whether or not I'm a high flyer among all those people who came to Clark County to escape or find a new life. I don't have to be a showgirl or drive a pink Cadillac. I know how to find shade in the holes that keep me out of the heat, and I'll always be a creature of sand and sun. That's what those scars on my thighs tell me, the ones where I once lost a mass of what covered me, my skin lost to that unholy, yet holy landscape.

All of us are from a specific geography, captured in indelible memories, sights, smells, and sounds. It's useful to know why you've become the person standing in your shoes and to ask what and who you are. There could be a desert, a rise of mountains, the flatness of plains, or the swell of ocean in your history. The smells, the angles of light, the grass or no grass, snow, or too much sun. Maybe you were surrounded by water or by sand. Maybe green fields.

Unwind it. Understand it. Tell your story as I've told mine in so many ways. At least tell this story to yourself. Tell of the places where you wander in your thoughts, even if you're not aware you're wandering.

Acknowledgments

These essays span thirty-plus years of essay writing, first begun at *Utah Holiday* magazine, edited by Paul Swenson. My gratitude to him for enthusiastically nurturing my interest in thought pieces and for publishing them as well. I also wish to thank Francois Camoin, David Kranes, and Franklin Fisher, my fine writing teachers at the University of Utah who believed in the work I was doing. There were the Associated Writing Program annual meetings headed by Liam Rector and David Fenza. And then, Writers at Work, a Utah writers' conference (James Thomas and Dolly Makoff, founders), which I helped produce. These both provided the opportunity to mix with and learn from editors, publishers, agents and other writers such as Ai Bei from mainland China and Amy Tan from San Francisco. And how could I forget my colleagues in the Writing Program at Vermont College of Fine Arts (where I taught for nineteen years) who inspired me in so many ways? Special kudos to them for their influence: Leslie Ullman, Gladys Swan, Jack Myers, Larry Sutin, Laurie Alberts, Abby Frucht, David Jauss, David Wojahn, Rick Jackson, Betsy Scholl, Mary Ruefle, Xu Xi, Nance Van Winckel, and Natasha Saje. I also thank my writing colleagues in Denver—

Harrison Candelaria Fletcher and Mary Domenico—and in Park City, Utah—Michele Morris and Lyn McCarter—for their opinions and ideas about newly written essays as well as about the discipline of writing itself. All in all, I thank the countless people who have enlarged my thinking, some of whom appear in these essays, more than many of them imprinted on my mind.

I've traveled a long road away from the Mojave Desert, which played such a large part in who I've become, but that desert will always be part of me and part of my response to issues of the day. Thank you, sand, stone, and wind for your immutable guidance.

The author is grateful to the following journals and anthologies for publishing several of the essays in this book.

"The Desert, Waiting", *upstreet 16*, Summer 2020

"Oh, Say Can You See", from *How I Got Cultured: A Nevada Memoir* (winner of the AWP Prize for Creative Nonfiction, 1991; co-winner of the Andy Adams Prize for Short Fiction, University of Utah, 1982)

"Great Basin DNA", *Weber: The Contemporary West*, Fall 2014

"An Ode to the Mojave", *Transcontinental Reflections on the American West: Work, Images and Sounds Beyond Borders*, Portal Editions, UK, 2015

"The Precarious Walk Away from Mormonism, All the Time with a Stitch in My Side", *Dialogue: A Journal of Mormon Thought*, Fall, 1996

"The Knife Handler", *Agni 71*, Spring 2010; Cited as Notable in *Best American Essays* and *Best American Travel Writing*, 2011

"Sweetgrass", *upstreet 5*, 2009; Cited as Notable in *Best American Essays*, 2010

"At the Cannery", *Dialogue: A Journal of Mormon Thought*, Summer 2009; winner of the Eugene England Memorial Essay Award, 2009

"Dancing with the Sacred, Three Parts", *numbercinqmagazine.com*, April 2012

"The Nested Self", originally "The Fictional 'I' in Non-fiction" in *Saying the Unsayable: Creative Writing Instruction and Insight from the Vermont College of Fine Arts Faculty*, Writer's Digest Press, 2008

"Responsibility: The Essential Gesture", originally "Writing as an Act of Responsibility" in *Dialogue, A Journal of Mormon Thought*, Spring 2008. Re-printed as the Introduction to *The Best of Mormonism 2009*, Curelom Books, Salt Lake City, Utah, 2009

ABOUT THE AUTHOR

Phyllis Barber is an award-winning author of nine books, including *The Desert Between Us*, *Raw Edges*, and *How I Got Cultured*. Winner of the AWP Prize for Creative Nonfiction, she has published essays and short stories in *North American Review*, *Crazyhorse*, and *Kenyon Review*. She has been cited as Notable in *The Best American Essays* and in *The Best American Travel Writing*. In 2005, Barber was inducted into the Nevada Writers' Hall of Fame. Barber has taught at the Vermont College of Fine Arts and the University of Utah's Osher Institute. She lives in Park City, Utah.

ABOUT THE COVER ART

Cover art by Hallie Rose Taylor
Virga, 2018

Hallie Rose Taylor is a multidisciplinary artist and writer. Her human experience is channeled into work which serves to translate the transcendent to the graspable and vice versa, through exploration of symbol and metaphor. Born in Salt Lake City, Utah, Hallie always engaged with art in some form: drawing and painting, dabbling in several musical instruments, and finally dedicating herself to modern dance. After a tragedy which took her away from the dance world for several years, she eventually came back around to visual art, pursuing illustration for commercial and client-based projects. Over the course of nearly a decade spent in Austin, Texas, she built a more intensive and spiritually connected art practice, including writing—which she has always done with a fervor but never found a place for. Her early world of movement helps her to dance among all of these approaches, carrying her ceaseless exploration of philosophical, psychological, ecological, and spiritual ideas.

Learn more at www.hallierosetaylor.com.

TORREY HOUSE PRESS

Voices for the Land

The economy is a wholly owned subsidiary of the environment, not the other way around.

—Senator Gaylord Nelson, founder of Earth Day

Torrey House Press publishes books at the intersection of the literary arts and environmental advocacy. THP authors explore the diversity of human experiences with the environment and engage community in conversations about landscape, literature, and the future of our ever-changing planet, inspiring action toward a more just world. We believe that lively, contemporary literature is at the cutting edge of social change. We seek to inform, expand, and reshape the dialogue on environmental justice and stewardship for the human and more-than-human world by elevating literary excellence from diverse voices.

Visit www.torreyhouse.org for reading group discussion guides, author interviews, and more.

As a 501(c)(3) nonprofit publisher, our work is made possible by generous donations from readers like you.

Torrey House Press is supported by Back of Beyond Books, the King's English Bookshop, Maria's Bookshop, the Jeffrey S. & Helen H. Cardon Foundation, the Sam & Diane Stewart Family Foundation, the Barker Foundation, Diana Allison, Klaus Bielefeldt, Laurie Hilyer, Kitty Swenson, Shelby Tisdale, Kirtly Parker Jones, Robert Aagard & Camille Bailey Aagard, Kif Augustine Adams & Stirling Adams, Rose Chilcoat & Mark Franklin, Jerome Cooney & Laura Storjohann, Linc Cornell & Lois Cornell, Susan Cushman & Charlie Quimby, Betsy Gaines Quammen & David Quammen, the Utah Division of Arts & Museums, Utah Humanities, the National Endowment for the Humanities, the National Endowment for the Arts, the Salt Lake City Arts Council, the Utah Governor's Office of Economic Development, and Salt Lake County Zoo, Arts & Parks. Our thanks to individual donors, members, and the Torrey House Press board of directors for their valued support.

Join the Torrey House Press family and give today at www.torreyhouse.org/give.